Full Face to God

Full Face to God

HÉLÈNE DICKEN

WITH A FOREWORD BY
THE BISHOP OF WILLESDEN

LONDON

S·P·C·K

1971

First published in 1971
by S.P.C.K.
Holy Trinity Church
Marylebone Road
London NW1 4DU

Made and printed in Great Britain by
The Talbot Press (S.P.C.K.), Saffron Walden, Essex

SBN 281 02598 3

TO

M. W. and K. G. T.

BISHOPS OF THE CHURCH,

with gratitude for help and encouragement
over many years

Contents

ACKNOWLEDGEMENTS

Thanks are due to the following for permission to quote from copyright sources:

John M. Watkins: *Adornment of Spiritual Marriage*, by J. Van Ruysbroek, ed. Evelyn Underhill

S.C.M. Press: *Honest to God*, by J. A. T. Robinson

The passage by Archbishop Anthony Bloom on p. 52 is from an address given privately and is quoted by permission.

Foreword

One characteristic of much contemporary Christian thought is its impatience with history. In the case of dogmatic theology the result has been that we have been asked to travel down roads which have already been shown to be dead ends. A different situation obtains with regard to the theology and practice of the spiritual life. Indifference to the teaching of the Masters of the spiritual life, which has perhaps been more marked inside the Church than outside, has resulted in attempts to recover some of their methods of spirituality but without the discipline and understanding of man's relationship to God which are their indispensable accompaniment. That the methods should be revived is hardly surprising since the Masters possess an understanding of human nature which is of perennial significance. Such understanding, however, springs from their awareness of God, whom man is created to adore in loving obedience. In contrast with the present attitude, which often seems to try and judge God by his usefulness to man, the Masters insist that he is both consuming fire and infinite love whom man learns to know by dying in Christ to his own self-centredness and living in a spirit of dependence and obedience.

Mrs Dicken first gives us an invaluable analysis of the present situation. There follows a powerful plea for the recovery of the contemplative attitude in the life of the contemporary Christian, both in personal direction and in liturgical worship. Mrs Dicken makes the point very clearly that the essence of the contemplative life lies in man's attitude towards God, not merely in the methods which are adopted. It is sometimes thought that contemplatives despise creation and are concerned with an unbiblical and purely spiritual approach to God. Mrs Dicken's stimulating discussion of analogies from the work of the artist and poet makes it clear that the true contemplative by insisting on seeing creation only in its relation to its Creator in a spirit of detachment, is enabled to see and appreciate its true potential.

As one who was trained in a scientific discipline I must gently protest against Mrs Dicken's statement that contemplative experience shares no common language with modern scientific attitudes. What she says about the limits of the scientific approach is true, but I think she overlooks the fact that the scientist has to accept the "givenness" of the external world which he seeks to investigate. This necessity for obedience to fact, accounts, I believe, for the way in which it is often easier to speak about the things of God to the Science Sixth in a school than to the Arts Sixth for whom so much seems to be a matter of opinion.

I am very glad to be able to commend this book. I hope that it will be read widely and do much to recall the Church to the fact that the only justification for our existence is to be found in God whom we are created to know and adore and with whom we are to live in communion both in this world and in that which is to come.

✠ GRAHAM WILLESDEN

Introduction

At the present time publishers and authors alike are aware that traditional spirituality is out of favour. This was not the case ten years ago. Between 1957 and 1963, David Knowles' *English Mystical Tradition*, Martin Thornton's *English Spirituality*, and paper-back editions of Walter Hilton and the Life of St Teresa all appeared and sold readily. The publication of *Honest to God* in 1963 marked something of a watershed, after which for some considerable time the "God debate" tended to make best-sellers of books which appeared to contribute significantly to this latter argument. From this new line in theology has stemmed a new approach to spirituality, and in this different climate the older classics of devotional literature have seemed at the least irrelevant.

There is much conviction that these fresh winds on the ecclesiastical scene have blown away a lot of cobwebs. On the other hand, as many parish priests know, there has been bewilderment and distress at less articulate levels in the Church. In 1968 a *Times* article by Walter James[1] referred to "the forgotten men and women in the Church of England" as being profoundly worried and upset, and not overmuch impressed, by the spirit of the age to which so many of the rethinkers of the Christian faith would have them accomodate themselves.

Meanwhile the organizational side of the Church's life has geared up to a quite remarkable extent. An almost feverish activity has multiplied commissions and committees in an effort to deal simultaneously with half a dozen major matters of doctrine and administration. In the words of American astronauts, all systems are now go.

And yet despite all this freshness of approach and reassessment there has been no widespread recovery of Christian faith and practice. Nor has the Church's new-style dialogue with the secular world improved its popular image in ways which might have been expected. Even the most sanguine observer of the current scene in the world of entertainment, for example, cannot but feel that the relaxation of censorship has led to a quite unprecedented low-water mark in the representation not only of sexual perversion and sensual titillation but also of the crudest blasphemy. When a noted actor-manager publicly announces that he is appalled at the standards of the commercial theatre,[2] and when young dancers and actresses turn down parts for which they are financially desperate because they refuse to take all their clothes off, there is not much doubt that Christian standards in general cut little ice with a very large public.

It is hardly surprising that many clergy are oppressed and disheartened. Even those radicals who have been most confident that they possessed the contemporary key to effective pastoral action have on occasion publicly proclaimed their own failure.

Some people, and not only traditionally minded theologians, are convinced that the only key to the Church's situation is a true spirituality, understood as the demanding theory and practice of a life progressively renewed and changed by the grace and love of God.

The moral concern of the new theologians themselves has made it clear that the call for personal integrity is an essential feature of their message. They have thus focussed fairly and squarely on the individual's personal responsibility, decrying by contrast, as they have every right to do, a merely conventional adherence to an ecclesiastical system, however venerable. But there are distinct differences of opinion as to the manner of achieving integrity and exercising responsibility. The new theology stresses the notions of involvement and commitment, but the involvement is expected to be with the secular world and the commitment to our fellow-men within it. The new spirituality has a strong this-worldly emphasis.

Has the new climate in the Church failed to bring in a better harvest because, in our concern with the world, we have not adequately driven home the relevance of relationship with its Creator? Have we, in other words, failed to appreciate the realistic importance of spiritual discipline, worship, and wonder?

The Church has an obvious mission to the world at large and must clearly make use of psychological and sociological insights in pursuing it, mustering its resources to combat injustice and want wherever it can usefully intervene. But its basic mission is still the spreading of the good news of salvation, and its deepest purpose that of helping individuals to make the fact of salvation operative in their own lives.

A valid spiritual theology then must concern itself most precisely with the development both at individual and corporate level of the crucial relationship between man and God. It will not offer temporary panaceas or placebo techniques of accommodation to secularism. It will lay its major emphasis on the nature of God and the nature of man, and on techniques not of mutual human accommodation but of worship and conformity to the divine.

It seems to be in this field that our teaching and practice has worn dangerously thin. John Robinson thought that the Church in our time was being called not merely to restate traditional orthodoxy in modern terms, but to throw into the melting-pot "the most fundamental categories of our theology".[3] Perhaps it bears suggestion, now that the dust of theological debate over the last few years is beginning to settle somewhat, that it is less our categories of theological thinking which are primitive than our ways of coming to grips with these categories in our daily lives.

A couple of years ago, some students of theology were asked, during a discussion group on prayer, to record anonymously on a scrap of paper the amount of time given to private prayer each day. The average proved on investigation to be six and a half minutes. And yet they were spending hours a day thinking, writing, and talking *about* God, struggling to deal both academically and personally with the flood of new theology and pastoral re-thinking which pours from the presses. These were students sophisticated far beyond the average in their religious interests and orientation. A less academic group, again young committed Christians, voiced the general conclusion that daily prayer formed no part of their programme, being replaced by vague thoughts and feelings *about* God and religion in general. One does not question in the least the sincerity of the people who gave these replies. But one cannot avoid the conclusion that so flimsy a foundation of personal relationship with a personal God is not really what Christianity is all about. No amount of academic expertise or of social involvement can in the long run be a substitute for a vital and progressive relationship with God.

It is not my intention either to write a justification of spiritual theology or to study in any depth techniques of the spiritual life. Excellent books are available on both these subjects. My aim is much more limited. It is to consider the relevance of the contemplative rather than the discursive approach in religious life to some of the current problems which face the Church and the individual Christian. I hope also to suggest that, despite the heavy scientific and technological bias of our present civilization, there are spheres of thought and culture, not immediately related to religious themes, where the contemplative approach is both understood and valued.

If a modern composer of the stature of the late Roberto Gerhard can define the major aim of a great work of art as being to produce "that stage of perfect detachment whereby originator and perceiver find access to a part of themselves where all are essentially the same, but where their common ground is far beyond the plane of superficial social conformity",[4] it would seem that the language of the Christian contemplative tradition is not wholly at variance with some of the profounder aspects of contemporary culture.

I

A Society Adrift

The diagnosis of modern ills is a favourite parlour game at all
levels of society. The needs of the people, of the community,
of young folk, of the individual are continually debated and
discussed; and there has been a significant expansion in
departments of sociology and social administration in all our
universities. Unless the Church too looks at the needs she is
supposed to meet, she is unlikely to commend herself either
as the guardian of a faith or even as a therapeutic society,
though it is well to remember that people's declared aims are
not always consonant with their real needs.

In this country, and in other highly sophisticated and industrialized areas, there are certain factors which strongly differentiate contemporary life from much that has gone before.
One of these is surely the quite unprecedented growth of the
means of communication. No national disaster or politically
motivated horror fails to make front page news and achieve
international coverage. The sheer weight of accumulated
suffering and despair can become intolerable for compassionate individuals of sensitive conscience. For some, the spate of
communication leads to a deadening of response, creating in
its turn a deep undercurrent of guilt. In others, the neural
strain leads more rapidly to crisis situations and mental disintegration.

The increasingly dense texture of modern urban life creates
its own additional pressures. The increased tempo of activity,
the complication of administrative procedures from which
even the simplest family unit cannot escape and the rising

level of mere sound are all disruptive factors. A medical journal devoted an article quite recently to the increase of noise in the kitchen, where automatic washers, tumbler-dryers, ventilation systems, electric mixers, and washing-up machines create a situation in the home where a wife may well be lonely, but rarely quiet. Here again people react differently. Some get so used to background noise that they cannot work without it. Others find it nerve-racking or even insupportable.

A further situation factor is the growing permissiveness of modern life. In all spheres, there is a weakening of mutual human respect and confidence, so that traditional loyalties and standards seem to be crumbling under the onslaught of experiment. Social and personal patterns are extremely fluid, and even in apparently stable societies and groupings, the trumpet seems to give a very uncertain sound.

Meanwhile, the figures for the incidence of various kinds of mental and nervous disease, for delinquency in the young and for violent crime in general, rise constantly.

There was a desperate seizure of the image of a new Elizabethan age when the present Queen succeeded to the throne, and there are sudden surgent popular phenomena like the "I'm backing Britain" campaign of the devaluation crisis, but on the whole a mixture of depressed aimlessness and cynicism is the prevalent mood of the country. Personal values suffer and frustrating situations multiply.

The technological age, while it guarantees for many in the affluent society a degree of comfort and material security hitherto unknown, is also subconsciously feared as an actual or potential affront to human dignity. Massive industrial organization often leaves little room for value judgements or appreciation of personal skills. Books like *The Hidden Persuaders* show that, even as consumers, we are already subject to levels of manipulation of which we are completely unaware. As taxation rises to new heights, we are even less able to choose channels of benevolence than to choose a brand of butter. Our standards of thrift and self-reliance are undermined by the less fortunate aspects of the welfare state. Our children are channelled through an immense educational machine which frequently changes its objectives less for reasons of genuine educational good than for political advantage or economic expediency. A woman may soon find herself divorced, against her own will, to the prejudice of her own financial security, and in defiance of strongly held principles.

The desire "to be somewhat" is a natural corollary of this depression of the individual, and some of the behaviour we readily class as anti-social may arise from just this desire to assert oneself in the face of mass pressures. Philosophies affect the man in the street far more than he realizes, especially in an age of popular newspaper culture. The theatre-going public is fed on a diet of existentialist plays and "non-happenings", and the general climate of purposelessness filters down to the bored and frustrated young lout who beats up an elderly man to see what it feels like.

Even the individual's relationship with his God, traditionally rooted in personal commitment and personal experience, is in danger of being undermined. Theologians debate a non-cognitive view of religious language, and their discussions are more easily popularized than comprehended. The man in the street may be puzzled to discover that God is at least half-dead. The Christian struggling with his prayers is all too readily persuaded that the exercise is pointless and out-of-date.

Perhaps the final and most ironical example of this desire for individuality is shown in suicide, humanly speaking the ultimate act of self-destruction. Social psychiatrists, studying the alarming problem of suicide in overcrowded cities, have no hesitation in saying that a considerable proportion, especially among the young, do not really want to die. By a desperate appeal for help, by a gamble with death, they intend the drama of attempted suicide to be a means of communication with those around them, a pitiable assertion of their need to be considered as an individual. And one needs to remember that in Edinburgh, for instance, one in ten among cases of any degree of seriousness which passed through the doors of the local major hospitals in 1967 were attempted suicides. It is now estimated that 50,000 people in the British Isles tried to end their lives in the course of 1970, and that the figure is likely to rise by 10% annually.

There is another side of the coin. The individual needs to be aware of his identity. He then needs to enrich and fulfil himself by learning to fit in, finding himself in a recognizable situation in a recognizable grouping. Urbanization was already undermining the sense of community before ever modern permissiveness began to undermine family structures. Current methods of educational administration can add to this sense of social dislocation. Most children who used to go to a village school first left home to move into an environment which had been a familiar part of the life of the village all the time they were growing up to school age. Nowadays, the passion for educational efficiency and opportunity can lead to the removal of groups of very young children from an essentially rural environment to a neighbouring colliery area where from nine in the morning until four in the afternoon, the five-year-old will be pressed into a background culture which is wholly foreign. Patterns of social adjustment cannot easily be formed of such recalcitrant situations.

Fluidity of population and the apparent ease with which the young make new lives for themselves in distant towns reproduce this same stress in adjustment later in life. Housing estates swarm with lonely and ill-adjusted wives, and with children bored for lack of genuine channels of discovery and adventure. Nor is the tragedy of the isolated "senior citizen" lessened by the pompous choice of official phraseology. The misuse of drugs by the unhappy elderly and middle-aged is a less dramatic but no less insistent problem of medical care than their misuse among young people. The thirty-six million prescriptions for drugs of all kinds signed in 1967 by the family doctor represent for the most part the discontents and ill-adjustments of ordinary people rather than the newsworthy excesses of the young.

Finally, it is perhaps not unduly fanciful to instance the need for that stimulus which at the lower end of the scale craves excitement and in more sophisticated areas of human aspiration craves enlightenment or illumination. It is soundly human to feel that there must be a place in life for the crest of the wave, the sudden lift of joy or flash of vision; and it is traditional to equate this stuff of creativity with the capacity to feel, perceive, and accept pain. But here contemporary modes of advertising do modern man, and woman even more so, a grave disservice. Whatever politicians may say about periods of grim endeavour, the advertisers and other mass media persist in overselling almost every known source of comfort and pleasure from a bar of soap to the sexual act itself. Thus, false expectations are continually aroused; and people are led to expect not, as Dame Julian put it, that in God's time "all shall be well and all manner of thing shall be well", but that here and now they have an indefeasible right to any comfort or advantage of which the man in the advertisement or the man next door finds himself possessed.

The awakening can be very rude indeed. Either nothing ever satisfies, and in a grey world light and colour become dependent upon cannabis, celluloid glamour, or false identifications; or very genuine present pleasures deteriorate in appeal because they are not evaluated realistically but are distorted by the rosy glow of magazine romance. Either way the individual finds himself bereft of contentment and peace of mind, increasingly incapable of living within either his financial or his emotional limits.

It is an encouragement that thousands and thousands of decent and reasonable people struggle with the mounting problems and pressures of our environment, and make positive contributions in all sorts of fields. But the magnitude of overall human need in industrialized countries, still more the near destitution in undeveloped lands, must convince us that we live in a world showing distinctly morbid symptoms. It is to this world that the Church must proclaim its message of life.

2

The Ark of God

———◆———

Many of the distressed and disillusioned do not look to the Church or to any concept of God for a solution or support. This book is in no sense an exercise in conversion technique aimed at persuading them to do so. It is rather a reflection on some of the answers the Church can offer to those who clearly do look to her to provide them. Christians must by definition look to God, and each Christian must look to the Church to meet the challenge of an increasingly high ratio of human need.

The Church of England is clearly aware of this, though perhaps sometimes more conscious of its mission to the un-converted than its mission to succour those already within. But the Church itself is in some confusion and disarray, and more alert to the need of mission than confident about its methods of pursuing it.

The notion of ministry, and therefore the pattern of train-ing for it, is under heavy pressure. However much the report *Theological Colleges for Tomorrow*, the Runcie Commission and the decisions of the House of Bishops look ahead to a streamlining of resources and an overall strategy, the fact remains that the theological colleges of today are in many cases thinly populated, accommodating only 834 men in 1970 as compared with 1,369 in 1965—and this despite the fact that less than ten years ago plans were being discussed for the provision of a new one on a university site because of pressure on places in existing ones.

Those working among young people in spheres of higher education see another aspect of the situation. Many of the excellent young men of clear Christian conviction who are such rewarding students in training colleges for teachers or in departments of social administration would ten years ago have been in theological colleges or in departments of theology, with the intention of proceeding to ordination. Now the wastage rate begins even before university age among those who cannot see the usefulness of the ordained ministry; among potential ordinands already in universities the wastage rate remains high; and, not long ago, one's year's intake of a theological college provided only two candidates for the diaconate. One does not begrudge to education and the social services the recruitment of these dedicated and competent young men; but there must be some disquiet that the call to spiritual welfare work has so few hearers.

Principals of theological colleges are keenly aware of the uncertainty among the students they do get, though not all of them would canvass the same solution. Indeed the students themselves frequently wish to pursue contradictory objectives. One entirely honest young man at a college which still fills most of its places complained bitterly of the conventional curate-at-a-tea-party image, despite the very considerable variety of work and activity available to him. Another at the same college was distressed to the point of leaving by the employment of certain contemporary and controversial techniques of psychological self-discovery and adaptation! Yet another came back from a different college after only one term in a state of considerable nervous strain and announced to students still at university, "They don't believe anything there. The Ministry is out. The Book of Common Prayer is out. Even the Bible is out".

These are clearly the exaggerated evaluations of worried young men, but it is worth remembering that they were survivors who had already stayed a long and difficult course. On the other hand there must be sympathy for Principals caught between commissions of enquiry and investigation from above and a groundswell of discontent at student level.

The sense of confusion and uncertainty which affects a considerable proportion of ordinands neatly pinpoints the situation in the Church as a whole. The vocation of every ordinand is nurtured first of all at parochial level, and he will subsequently be drawn into close contact with the teaching and pastoral office of the Church in almost every context.

Despite the activities of the clergy in specialized situations, the parish is still the basic unit of Christian discipleship. Here for most people is still the focal point of their effort to synthesize Christian faith and Christian living. However far the pattern of group ministries or part-time priesthood may develop, incumbents of individual churches, with or without clerical or ancillary staff, will still be key figures in the presentation of the Church's answers to the problems of life. And at the moment they are often grossly overburdened men.

The report *Theological Colleges for Tomorrow* rightly stresses that, at the merest economic level, "the parish church and the circle of worshippers attending it, who naturally form the core of the incumbent's ministry, often turn out to be dominated by questions of financial survival."[1] Hence the activist succession of fund-raising schemes which affords the most widely recognized image of parochial life.

If conscientious members of a local church have any energy left when they have repaired the fabric, rehung the bells or, most urgent of all in many country districts, overhauled the heating system and paid the inevitably heavy bills for its maintenance, they are exhorted to take part under the leadership of their pastor in study groups and projects which follow one another with bewildering speed and a fine variety of cryptic alphabetical titles. Bulky questionnaires on a medley of subjects fall through the vicarage letter-box, quotas and costs go inexorably up. More deadly still, the parish priest is assailed on all sides by the suggestion that his function is largely superseded on the one hand by social services, on the other by laity participation.

The burden becomes crushing indeed when activism crowds out the time for study and above all for prayer. It is interesting in this context to note that the present Bishop of St Albans, formerly Principal of Cuddesdon, in a newspaper comment on the Theological College Report, said that he missed in it "the note of withdrawal".[2] It is dangerously absent today at the parochial level.

Moreover, by the very nature of his work, the parish priest is a somewhat isolated man and greatly needs the support, sympathy, and understanding of those who share his specialized vocation. His bishops are often too overburdened with administrative chores to give it. And recent discussions and debates have sometimes so tended to sharpen the outlines of commitment and conviction among the parochial clergy that there is a wariness and uncertainty even in their dealings with each other. This distressing phenomenon bears hardly on those who have worked together for years and now feel that the old candour and confidence is lacking.

Nor is the generaton gap confined to the laity. There are angry young men in the ministry as well as outside it, and young clergy who feel themselves confined and limited by pastoral attitudes they deem out-worn. Older men wonder if experience counts for nothing, and find it difficult to steer a steady course between rigid conservatism and too facile accommodation.

The laity of the Church are bound to suffer from disorientation among the clergy, as well as having their own distinctive problems. The emphasis on lay participation and the priesthood of the laity invites them into a rewarding partnership in the life of the Church. But the more active they become in its councils and pastoral mission, the more they are caught up into problems of a theological nature. Simple solutions to dogmatic questions and problems of ecumenical policy come more easily to the lay mind than to those whose theological training has made them aware of less obvious implications. The very fact of greater lay participation may itself drive a wedge of misunderstanding and irritation between pastor and people.

In the long run, there should be incalculable gains from this new dialogue on so many fronts, between young and old, between Anglicans, Roman Catholics, and Nonconformists, between clergy and laity. But in periods of transition there is bound to be friction and fear, which can only really be resolved by patience and charity, the traditional stock-in-trade of the committed Christian.

Perhaps then the most significant need of the parochial clergy is for theological support and sympathetic guidance from those in key positions at diocesan and university level. Secularist philosophies and modes of thought are didactic, pervasive, and extremely articulate. The parish priest must know where to look for informed help in stating the theological background of his own commitment and of his work among his own people. His parishioners are continually assailed by all the resources of secularism, whether they are aware of them or not. He cannot help even the least sophisticated of them unless he himself is supported in love and faith by his pastors in God, and the theologians of his Church.

3

Remedial Debate?

What kind of theological support is on offer today to the perplexed priest? Dr Mascall has clearly defined the task of the Christian theologian as that of "relating the revealed datum of Christian truth, final, absolute, and fundamentally permanent as he must by his Christian commitment believe it to be, to the essentially incomplete, relative and constantly changing intellectual framework of the world in which he lives".[1] Is contemporary theological debate firmly anchored upon this basic duty?

The details of the impact of Barth and Brunner, of Bultmann, Bonhoeffer, and Tillich, and latterly of Van Buren upon the theological climate of this country—and the conclusions John Robinson and others drew from their writings—have been discussed and debated in every possible medium of communication from the *News of the World* to the parochial pulpit. It would be pointless and wearisome to labour over them again.

But there seem to be certain aspects of the explosion of post-war theological controversy which are particularly germane to the purpose of this book.

The new theology has seemed at times to be so clearly successful in a take-over bid for the mind of the Church that the origins of some of the concepts which influenced it have been obscured. One of its declared aims is to come to grips with the contemporary situation. Its advocates rightly expect the Church to consider very seriously its situation *vis-à-vis* the secular world. But in so doing they have turned with

understandable admiration to theologians who found themselves in most direct and harrowing conflict with secular pressures. They thus tended perhaps to forget that, diverse and
distinct as the contributions of these theologians undoubtedly
were, the ethos from which they all drew inspiration was in
fact continental Protestantism. Thus the clear doctrinal posi-
tion of the Anglican Church, whose formularies do not reflect,
and were never meant to reflect, continental Protestantism,
has been somewhat obscured and undervalued in the debate.
This is most noticeable in the field of moral teaching, and
where attitudes to the Scriptures and forms of the Church are
concerned.

Moreover the dependence of the new theology on definite
and systematized philosophical outlooks should not be over-
looked. Bultmann's processes of thought are inseparable from
existentialist philosophy, and Van Buren uses the conclusions
of linguistic analysis to develop his non-cognitive view of
religious language and belief. The point to be noted is that
both these approaches are in themselves reactions against
nineteenth-century systems, and that, in the philosophical
world, reactions are already developing in their turn to existentialism and linguistic analysis.

Clearly then what the new theologians genuinely have to
offer is what reformers have so often offered us in the past
—a redistribution of emphasis, meeting and influenced by
certain definite current situations. The whole contribution of
the new theology gets out of proportion if it is wildly and
often uncomprehendingly presented as a radical reconstruc-
tion based on a mythical notion that man has come of age.

A true sense of historical perspective would surely temper
any exultant triumphalism in making use of the notion that
man has come of age. But here we perhaps meet a disquieting
feature of the new theology, which it shares, equally disquiet-
ingly, with the world at large. A sense of history has at the
moment a rapidly diminishing credit balance in this country.
Statistics support this view. In the university world, for example, posts asking for special qualifications in modern Euro-

pean history, Asian and African studies, American and recent
Eastern European history abound, but the career opportunities open to medievalists are shrinking. This could be claimed
as a victory for realism in historical studies, as against what
has been called the arid professionalism which regards history
as made for the historian. But we dare not lose sight of the
disciplined study of the past. We need to add the dimension
of time to the three dimensions we commonly perceive.

The urgent and praiseworthy desire of some present-day
theologians to speak significantly to the world they live in
seems to blind them on occasion to the dimension of time.
This is partly a natural consequence of their concentration
upon man in his immediate existential situation. One cannot
say everything on every page. But perhaps Eric Mascall has
a point when he talks of Bultmann's "uncritical lumping together as myth of anything unacceptable to the twentieth
century."[2] Theological debate becomes alarmingly un-
anchored if it forgets that the key feature of all theology is
revelation, a historical faith which can be restated in the idiom
of the age, and is open to new contingent emphases, but is
not patient of change which would alter its very nature.
Heresy is an ugly word and is associated with ugly manifesta-
tions, but, shorn of its emotive content, its authoritarian excesses, and its demonstrations of violence, it is a way of
saying "we have been down this way before and have found
it a dead end." So, when there are those among the new
theologians who seem to wish to reject the whole supernatural frame of reference of the Christian faith, some of us
cannot escape the suspicion that this is indeed one of the blind
alleys which have been thoroughly explored in the past.

In fact, in asking what kind of theological support the
clergy and more sophisticated laity are being given at the
present day, the issue of the supernatural is crucial.

What do we mean by the supernatural? Surely, as Eric
Mascall says, "that body of thought and activity which sees
man's life 'in this world' as deriving from 'another world' and
his final destiny as lying in that 'other world' and beyond

bodily death".[3] This definition would appear to have Scriptural warranty and to be clearly consonant with Anglican doctrine. The fact of revelation and the existence of grace bring the action of the supernatural within the confines of the natural, and Christian life will be by definition a life of personal relationship with God, lived out in time but oriented towards the eternal. The command to love one's neighbour derives from the command to love God; and there will be a wholly literal and factual sense in which the Christian is not "of this world".

Against this, the new theology tends to set a concentration on man in his actual situation here and now. It revalues the revelation of Christ, laying less stress on the Son of God and more on the "man for others". It can even be held to look suspiciously at basic and traditional religious activities as promoting a withdrawal *from* the world which hinders the search for God *in* the world. Derivatives of this approach, some less justified than others, include a full or partial rejection of "institutional religion", an intolerance of any attitude which can be regarded as inward-turned pietism, and a fundamental impatience with any ethical system which is not situational.

Harvey Cox's book *The Secular City* presses the arguments to their logical conclusion. The Church is no longer the guardian of revelation or of the means of grace, nor can it derive transcendental claims from a transcendental function. It is indeed the shock-troop of God, but primarily because its programme of action is humanist and very much of this world, and its purpose the violent engagement in society at every crisis point.

If this is to be the strategy of the people of God, then the concept of spirituality only saves itself from becoming out-of-date by literally turning itself inside out. God is vindicated by man's action, rather than man justified by God's salvation.

There is an interesting difference of approach between two paper-backs with similar titles, published before and after the explosion of popular theological debate which followed the publication of *Honest to God*.

Christian Spirituality Today was edited by the Archbishop of Canterbury and published in 1961, being a series of essays contributed to the *York Quarterly* between 1959 and 1960. *Spirituality for Today*, edited by Eric James and published in 1968, is the Report of the Parish and People Conference held in Durham in the Autumn of 1967.

In the earlier book, The Archbishop defines Christian spirituality as the Christian's whole life, seen however "not as an earthly activity which his relation to God assists, but as essentially a relation to God expressed in his earthly activity".[4] The papers in *Spirituality for Today* are not all of a piece, but Dr Harry Guntrip is one author among several who take a very different line. He states categorically that spirituality can no longer be defined as otherworldliness. He feels that the word, and the concept lying behind it, carries no conviction. "We cannot", he continues, "even raise the question of a spiritual world; it would have no meaning, unless we can find spirituality right here, in the very stuff and texture of our present material existence".[5]

This is more than just a different way of looking at things. Though one cannot doubt the burning sincerity with which it is said, it surely represents a reversal of the fundamental point of view of traditional spirituality that the secular is only meaningful in terms of the supernatural. It tends to narrow the vision of the Church, confining its purposes within the restrictive limits of modern technocratic society. Sundered thus from the dimension of eternity, the most extreme forms of new theology are understandably reduced to the marking down of selected doctrines as loss-leaders to revitalize the public image of the Faith.

Is it really credible that, within the eight years lying between the publication of these two books, traditions deriving from the experience of Christian living and teaching over nearly two thousand years should suddenly become obsolete? Is it not perhaps that some of our new theologians and new moralists in the Church of England, influenced by certain aspects of continental Protestantism and latterly of American theological speculation which are out of context in the Anglican tradition and in many ways totally unrepresentative of it, have in fact seriously misunderstood some of the basic attitudes of traditional spirituality?

Much careful expository work has indeed been done recently, and in our own Church, in the field of spiritual theology. But these still small voices are not easily heard in a climate influenced by positivist philosophy, massive scientific and technological advance, and the uncritical popularization of the demythologizing tendencies of recent Biblical scholarship. I believe that the time has come to listen more attentively to what the spiritual masters are really saying about the quality of living and the relationship between God and man, between this world and the next.

We may well discover that what they have to teach us is basic to our understanding of God and of ourselves. We may then look with more attention at the contemplative attitude which both formed and instructed them, and find it by no means as esoteric and eccentric as we expected.

4

The Contemplative Attitude

DEFINITION

In speaking of the contemplative attitude I am not at this point referring specifically either to the prayer of contemplation or to the contemplative life. These are technical theological terms, indicating in the one case a highly developed form of Christian prayer which is pre-eminently the work of grace, in the other a life conditioned, either in or out of community, by that measure of withdrawal which encourages the development of such a prayer.

Rather I would define the contemplative attitude primarily as a response to God awakened by a loving, but not discursive, awareness of him as the sole and sovereign source of all that is; and secondly as a humble and awed acceptance of what that implies in our own personal life and destiny.

Unless in some measure this attitude characterizes our relationship with God, there will be no realism in our approach to him, and little fundamental stability in our relationships with men. But it is an attiude which matures slowly; spiritual growth is a much more gradual process than either physical or mental growth. As it grows, it will necessarily be matched by personal discipline of an increasingly searching kind. It is this fact above all which has imparted a faintly esoteric character to the word "contemplative", as if it concerned only initiates of some highly systematized pattern of Christian life, who were *ipso facto* out of touch with the contemporary situation.

The reverse is surely the case. The contemporary situation

would not exist if God had ceased to sustain his creation. To know and serve God with a pure intention—the perfect fruit of the contemplative attitude—will bring a man effectively and realistically face to face with any situation, however contemporary. But he will neither see the situation with the world's eyes, nor act in it in a way which the world can readily accept. His categories of relevance will lie far deeper than those of pragmatist or humanist, but his vision will be all of a piece because it stems from the vision of God.

For anyone, therefore, who has a belief in a personal God, whatever the terms in which the word "personal" may be defined, some sort of spiritual life is an imperative. The question as to what constitutes a valid spiritual life has of recent years been hotly debated. The answer must clearly be sought in terms of a relationship between man and his creator, between religion and life, which leads neither to a withdrawal from the world conceived in dualist terms nor to a wholesale secularization of outlook.

A quotation from John Robinson aptly illustrates one approach to this relationship which has become widely accepted—"the man who acknowledges the transcendence of God is the man who *in* the conditioned relationships of life recognizes the unconditional and responds to it in unconditional personal relationship".[1] He pushes this concept still further in asserting that God, since he is love, is encountered in his fullness only *between man and man*, and that the specific kind of "religious experience" which looms so largely in traditional spiritual theology is no more necessary to a basic and genuine encounter with God than a good ear for music is necessary to the good life. Harry Guntrip, in *Spirituality for Today*, offers a further definition: "religious experience is best expressed as the capacity to be most fully and personally alive to every aspect of our existence, the way a human being who is free to feel and love experiences his entire environing reality".[2]

Both men are obviously saying something which is partially

true; it is the sort of language which is readily and rightly seized upon to justify every type of Christian action within a secular framework.

But not only is it not the whole truth; it is the sort of half-truth which, ill-digested by the inexperienced enthusiast, is apt to lead to spiritual shipwreck and a fundamental loss of nerve.

A classic description of religious experience from a Roman Catholic writer phrases the matter very differently: "Christianity is seen to be a form of spiritual life in which our most personal, most interiorized relationship with God himself in his transcendent reality is fully recognized and *formally cultivated*".[3] Here Louis Bouyer is not afraid to suggest that a relationship with God needs to be consciously developed as the ground of a man's developing spiritual awareness, and the suggestion derives surely from the conviction that the ultimate purpose of man is to give glory to God. An individual so oriented will clearly be drawn increasingly to give himself to his fellow men in sacrificial love and labour. But the heart of his religious experience will be not activist, but contemplative, as befits a being who is not only, as Harry Guntrip phrases it, a "human being experiencing his entire environing reality", but also a child of God working out his salvation in terms of eternal life.

This latter attitude must be present to some degree in the simplest act of worship. The basic attitude of faith is wonder and worship; the basic concept of Christian life is the conforming of life to the requirements of faith. We cannot bypass this essential contemplative attitude; unless activity proceeds from worship and wonder and seeks first the glory of God, it will proceed from self-determination and worry and will seek first the advancement of man.

Is it perhaps at this crucial point that the new theology is failing us? Agonized, anxious involvement is only free from self if the agony is the agony of the Cross and the involvement a share in Christ's passion. These are not well-worn, conventional phrases no longer applicable to a society where moral concern is the ultimate test of sincerity; they express a sober theological truth, rooted in Scripture, validated time and again by the tradition and experience of the Church, and the only final defence against the arid Pelagian conception of man as the captain of his soul, committed to the salvation of himself and all men by self-directed effort.

The contemplative attitude is thus humble, dependent, and penitent, because it gazes upon God as wholly other, not, be it noted, as the inspiration of a programme of social or any other sort of reform. David Knowles extends the dictionary definition of "contemplative" to a "prolonged and affective gaze upon an object of sight or thought",[4] and goes on to note the association of the word with the idea of repose. All these notions of humility, dependence, penitence, and repose are unfashionable today, and seem to suggest a timid, shrinking, distrustful, and uncreative withdrawal from the world : we forget that again and again these traits have characterized personalities whose ultimate achievements in fields of Christian action have been memorable and massive. The contemplative attitude is rooted upon experience of God, not upon experience of man, and contemplative awareness is deepened by the progressive discovery in prayer, sacrament, and worship, of a God who is himself a supremely personal being. In other words, this attitude stresses the fact that God made man in his own image, and it could never get the issue the wrong way round.

RELATIONSHIP WITH GOD

From this basic attitude spring several important considerations which have tended to be obscured by the current ferment of debate and discussion.

In the first place, it leads to an acceptance of God's action upon a personality as vital to that personality's growth. The individual will be seen to have an inescapable frame of reference, and that frame of reference is God—not a shadowy being dimly glimpsed, if at all, behind the concrete reality of the visible world, but a Reality solid, convincing and all-embracing.

The unbeliever will obviously take tentative steps towards reality and personal significance by extending the range and depth of his personal relationships, but the Christian by definition should not need either to defend his sincerity or seek a spurious self-confidence by insisting that he too must anchor himself primarily in communication between man and man.

If God is to act upon a personality, there must be a channel open to him, a means of awareness and response. Prayer therefore is not an optional extra, but the normal means of spiritual growth. It may be true, as Dean Coburn says, that "transcendent being, saintly lives, holy people, worshipping communities, the people of God, mean nothing to the minds of thousands of adult people",[5] but this is not an open invitation to Christians to be brain-washed by secularism—and often by teachers within the Church—into abandoning the doctrines of the faith and the spiritual disciplines which derive from them. John Coburn continues that, for many people today (and he specifically includes people within the Church) "any concept of spirituality which begins with God, Father, Son, and Holy Spirit is meaningless", but, if that becomes true of us as Christians, then in all fairness we can hardly pretend to offer God's answers to the world's need. If, on the other hand, it means something, then it means everything, and we cannot be ashamed to affirm that a right relationship to man presupposes a right relationship to God.

Relationships are made in awareness, and awareness of God is the fruit of prayer. This does not mean that prayer is to be practised and valued *because* it is a means to spiritual growth, but because it is the inescapable concomitant of a realistic relationship. And yet how rightly Bishop Wand says, "today more than ever we have to fight for our prayers, for the privilege of making them, and for the form in which they are normally cast", because "there are so many voices around us telling us that we are now grown-up and must no longer act like children".[6] There is indeed much talk nowadays about the need to find new ways of prayer to match the new theology and the new morality. It is coupled with the suggestion, more or less explicit, that traditional modes of instruction in prayer are ill-suited to our increasingly urbanized, secular and sophisticated environment, and may even do more harm than good.

The conviction grows that what is wrong is not traditional spirituality, but our own vast ignorance of what it is trying to say. We pick up odd phrases, odd concepts, and discard them because we fail to see them in context. The context of creation is the Creator, and a spiritual discipline and spiritual theology rooted in the contemplative attitude has far more to say to us in this present age than most superficial criticisms suggest.

SERVICE OF MAN

Let us take first an issue to which the modern Christian is peculiarly sensitive, the importance of Christian Action with or without the capital letters, and of all that is implied in the phrase, "Christ, the man for others".

The thoughtful Christian is fully aware that the inexorable pressure of technological civilization is in many ways a threat to the individual and to the old values of western society. He knows that much prosperity in fact coexists with much personal frustration, that there are vast areas of the world where populations exist in a state of poverty and misery to which technological advance has as yet brought no relief. He is moved therefore to real anxiety for the individual, both on the material and on the psychological level. He longs to establish conditions in which human dignity is protected alike from abject need and callous exploitation.

He finds no particular comfort in the fact that politicians are also aware that the technological revolution can threaten human personality, for their remedies are sometimes disconcertingly frank. In setting up a new productivity council, for example, in May, 1968, Barbara Castle expressed the hope that it would help to *humanize the technological revolution* by showing workers how these changes could *benefit them through their wage packets*".[7]

To a Christian, this attitude is as much an exploitation of the individual as the dehumanizing excesses of early industrialism; and any sort of theologian would recoil from the bland assumption that technological advance is humanized by being securely harnessed to self-interest.

The existentialist background of much of the new theology certainly ensures a concern for man's authentic being, not merely for his financial competence, and it displays a basic anxiety about the pressures exercised by a depersonalizing environment. Buber, for example, does not run away from man's everyday concerns, but endeavours to be open to the secular and to give it a profound significance by seeing it as the field of the divine–human encounter, where the I–Thou life of dialogue leads towards God, the eternal Thou.

Unfortunately, this thesis has of late been over-emphasized, and has emerged not only as "freedom for the secular," but also as freedom from religion, understood as including the institutions of religion, in the name of that to which religion points. So traditional worship and doctrine, and of course traditional spirituality too, are seen as irrelevant; and activity and involvement as the only proper Christian answer to an environment which must be humanized in the name of Christ. As Tillich himself emphasized, though Buber knew that the prophetic element in religion is safeguarded from legalism and moralism by the mystical element, the mystical element for him was an experience of the divine presence in the encounters and activities of daily life; he distrusted profoundly any interpretation of it which seemed to lead to an escape from reality and from the demands of the here and now. It is only a short further step to John Robinson's assertion that God is to be met not by an irrelevant special type of mystical experience but by an unconditional concern for other men. The traditional order of the two great imperatives, love God and love your neighbour, is reversed. The new attitude to Christian action is thus expressed—serve your neighbour and

you will love God. Service in fact is said to be the *only* way
to knowledge of God. "The way through to the vision of the
Son of Man and the knowledge of God, *which is the heart of
contemplative prayer*, is by unconditional love of the neighbour, of the nearest Thou to hand".[9]

In effect, the contemplative attitude, through all its mani-
festations from the simplest act of worship to the highest
point of the spiritual life of grace, with all its implications of
interior life and patient discipline of body, mind and spirit,
is left out of account. It is not even seriously repudiated: it is
merely by-passed as being not only an ineffective guide to
Christian action, but also as in itself the largely spurious
creation of medieval self-consciousness, serving only to mask
the message of grace as St Paul understood it, and as the
modern situation-conscious Christian can truly practise it. As
David Knowles remarked, as recently as 1967, "the body of
theoretical and practical teaching built upon the evidence of
the mystics and the writings of Fathers and theologians has
been almost entirely ignored by the purely empirical and
existentialist approach of modern thinkers".[10] And yet it is
not only an integral part of Christian teaching, grounded in
Scripture,[11] but itself offers the most integrated and most
clearly safeguarded series of answers to the problems of
Christian activity in the modern situation.

St Luke puts into the mouth of St Paul a classic description
of the nature of human dignity—"I declare unto you God that
made the world and all things therein . . . and hath made . . .
all nations of men for to dwell on all the face of the earth . . .
that they should seek the Lord . . . for in him we live and
move and have our being".[12] Man's dignity thus derives from
his place in creation, and souls exist in God and by God
and for God alone. God's infinite identity guarantees man's
identity in time and in eternity, and nothing in the world can
ever really be secular since the world itself is authenticated
and maintained by God's creative and redeeming love. Supernaturalism is thus the guarantee of that which we loosely call

the secular world, and can never be in opposition to man's basic needs.

The more therefore we contemplate the supernatural, the more we grasp the essence of the natural. To retire to contemplate God, to deepen our awareness by prayer and worship and the familiar modes of the spiritual life is not an irrelevant withdrawal, but a wholly practical method of seeking significant life not only for ourselves, but for and on behalf of all men. The Gospels invite to a life of continual self-sacrifice for others. The truly God-centred man will always be drawn to extraordinarily costly service *even if the means he chooses may seem otherworldly, remote, and withdrawn*. The aim is the coming of the Kingdom for all men, and *no-one* called to contemplate his Creator can by-pass his share in it.

There is no need to detail the self-surrendered service offered to their fellows by innumerable men and women of profound spiritual insight nourished by patient development of the contemplative attitude. The service is recognized and admired; but people are much less easily convinced that the attitude itself, leading invariably to some degree of withdrawal, whether day by day for serious prayer or for a lifetime in a religious order, is not only an essential part of the service rendered, but may itself be the most effective service of all.

And here we begin to establish the connection between what I have chosen to call the "contemplative attitude" and contemplative prayer or contemplation in the technical theological sense. Here nothing is pre-determined, and the action of grace upon a co-operating soul will lead not to a monotone of conformity, but to strongly individualized patterns of life and prayer. What is certain is that an attitude of worship and wonder, of awareness and response, will lead, at least intermittently, to a greater simplicity in prayer, a new experience of the presence of God. Some will be drawn further into the prayer of contemplation properly so called or to states of life associated with it, though it is necessary to note that the members of a contemplative order will not all find contemplation their normal way of prayer.

Nevertheless, the core of spiritual theology is the divine rhythm of contemplation and sacrificial service which is slowly but surely established in those whose life is profoundly rooted in God. Ruysbroeck speaks with startling directness and simplicity on this theme—"Our thought, our life, and our being are uplifted in simplicity, and made one with the Truth which is God. And therefore in this simple staring we are one life and one spirit with God: and this I call the contemplative life". But see where this leads: "The man who is sent down by God from these heights into the world is full of truth and rich in all its virtues. And he seeks not his own, but the glory of Him who sent him. And hence he is just and truthful in all things, and he possesses a rich generous ground which is set in the richness of God: and therefore he must always spend himself on those who have need of him; for the living fount of the Holy Ghost, which is his wealth, can never be spent. And he is a living and willing instrument of God, with which God works whatsoever He wills and howsoever He wills; and these works he reckons not as his own, but gives all the glory to God—and thus he possesses *a universal life*, for he is ready alike for contemplation and for action, and is perfect in both of them. *And none can have this universal life save the God-seeing man*".[13]

Such is the rhythm, but the detail of its establishment is the prerogative of God, not of man. And here we begin to see that the difference between the contemplative's attitude to the world's need and the attitude of the new theologian is something more than a quaint medievalism of expression.

The true contemplative is delivered by the very nature of his contemplative attitude from the *anxious* urgency which infects so much of the Church's action and discussion at the present time, insistent though her tasks of compassion and succour undoubtedly are. The contemplative has always been able to put time in its place because his element is eternity. Because God's victory over sin is already won in and through the incarnation, crucifixion, and resurrection of Christ, because God has all eternity to establish the fruits of it, we are delivered from the prevalent Pelagian presumption that we must "save" the Church or the world from this and that before it is too late. The alternative is not an apathetic acceptance of things as they are, but a vitality which uses the present with freedom because, as De Caussade so often pointed out, it is the one point of realistic contact with God. The *peaceful* performance of what appears to be our urgent duty in the present delivers us both from destructive and remorseful concern over what has been and from passionate anxiety over what will be. "Passionate involvement" in the sense in which the word "passionate" is generally used is apt to lead to short-lived enthusiasms and hasty decisions, because our horizons are so limited and our desire for self-justification so little disciplined by a real detachment from self. We are all familiar with the loss of nerve which follows upon the apparent failure of self-directed effort. There are many priests —and layfolk too—who struggle to get through to people with new techniques of worship and pastoral action; but it is when too much of self has gone into the effort that any partial failure can lead to a bitter sense of personal betrayal.

But if the word "passionate" be given its original meaning, "passionate involvement" can mean something very different from this often distracted and distracting activism. It can mean a degree of personal identification with the suffering of Christ which again is at the heart both of contemplative prayer and of any really fruitful contribution to the problems of the Church and the world. When a man, disciplined, detached and purified by his deepening relationship with God, is made aware of any situation where help is needed, then he will be compelled by that relationship to do with all his heart, mind, and will what he sees may be done.

But again and again the individual finds himself face to face with a problem where, humanly speaking, it appears that little can be done. In the increasing complexity of modern life, we feel often enough that we are powerless to influence situations which seem to offer no solution within our capacity. The contemplative's answer is literally the crucial one. He can suffer with Christ the burden of a world which, in seeking to please itself, separates itself from its only true contentment. He is thus delivered both from the sense of impotent isolation which haunts modern man, and from the creeping paralysis of final despair. The modern world is no less a world of suffering and death than Ruysbroeck's world, and the God-centred man has the same purpose now as then—to keep open the channels of Love's action by a complete conformity to him "who his own self bore our sins in his own body on the tree."

5

The Contemplative Life:
A Rationale of Withdrawal

———◆———

The most direct and obvious expression of contemplative prayer and self-offering on this crucial level is the contemplative life lived in community and characterized, especially in women's orders, by a considerable degree of enclosure. All religious vocations are of course the fruit of self-offering of a notably sacrificial kind, but communities of the mixed type, combining a measure of prayerful withdrawal with clearly demonstrable good works are more readily accepted by the world at large. In fact, only two or three years ago, a B.B.C. producer went on record as saying that nuns and small mammals were currently the peak attraction on television. The sentimentality of the "In a Monastery Garden" image has been replaced by a keen and sympathetic interest in communities devoting themselves to helping the outcasts and social misfits of every age and nationality.

But the contemplative order whose main work is prayer presents a much more disturbing and embarrassing image. Its validity stands or falls by the validity of the contemplative attitude; being in no way drawn into recognizable active service, the life so lived exhibits an inescapable clarity of function.

It is because the whole notion of withdrawal is so much under fire at the present time, both inside and outside the Church, that it is important to consider the relevance of this particular flowering of the contemplative attitude.

It is well, perhaps, to begin with one of the most devastating attacks delivered in recent years upon the Religious life in general and the principle of withdrawal in particular—an attack which at the time came from within.[1] Father Charles Boxer, a Dominican who has since left the Order, was invited to discuss the contribution of monasticism to spirituality in the world today at the Parish and People conference already referred to. He was not a member of a contemplative order; on the other hand, he was not only vowed by his particular vocation to a combination of the secluded, monastic life and pastoral, priestly work, but was also supported, as all his brethren are, by a Second Order of enclosed nuns, who live and pray within the almost complete enclosure typical of contemplative communities.

The essence of his attack is that religious communities have no relevance either in themselves or in the contemporary situation. In reference to the first point, he quotes with approval R. D. Laing's dictum that "we all know from our personal experience that we can only be ourselves in and through our world"—a statement which, as we have seen, is accurate only within a limited concept of selfhood and is barely applicable in terms of Christian theology. But Father Boxer derives from this statement the corollary that a monastery cannot be itself in and through its world because its world is anchored in the past, and has much the same validity today as veteran cars on a motorway. He then considers the function of the monk or nun as a "first-hand interpreter of God". He insists that, in the first place, the Religious cannot interpret his experience "because he does not experience God in the same sense as an interpreter experiences society", and, in the second place, he cannot usefully communicate any of his experience to the world because he is a person who is necessarily remote from society. Poised between a God he cannot interpret and a world with which he cannot communicate, he is imprisoned in a peculiar sort of artificial society. He is condemned either to a life "pervaded by superficial ordinariness", or to the long, slow agony of the critical reformer, leading in many cases to the "difficult and courageous step of leaving monasteries for life in the world".

Perhaps the provenance of his particular line of argument is most clearly shown when he finds the true contemporary purpose of what is left of monasticism in the help it can give to the Church as a whole "to go through the disintegration of its institutionalism and find once again its purpose in the world", for the Church needs "the disentegrating monastic wing as a model . . . of the future that threatens its existence in the world". Charles Boxer believes indeed that it is important that the Church should survive, but it cannot at the moment provide a relevant spirituality because it is morally alienated from contemporary life. "The Church", he asserts, "must be converted to the world before it can radicalize its spirituality". After this, we certainly hardly need to be told that he believes the answer to the problem of the relevance of monastic institutions to lie not in an attempt, a *theological* attempt, to make sense of the institutions as they are, but in critical, *existential* debate.

He is in fact concerned to detach the Religious life from its coherent theological framework, to judge it as a social institution by the degree of its adaptation to the world, and to value any spiritual contribution Religious may make by the extent to which they themselves have been "gradually undermined by the world's spirituality".

We may well ponder the significance of Charles Boxer's withdrawal from his Order. The fact that he is no longer a monk gives more rather than less point to his remarks. Similar strictures issue regularly from those still apparently living under obedience, but Charles Boxer's spiritual odyssey would seem to be at least the corollary of his expressed outlook.

Most Religious Orders in the Church of England are not yet exhibiting such dramatic signs of unease as those in the Roman Church. But the seeds of secularization are being quietly sown on our own ground; and already, in some quarters, an insistence upon the clear theological principles which are the foundation of the monastic life is unpopular.

Outreach has been praised at the expense of withdrawal in much current debate in the Anglican church; and this calls in question the essential concepts of the Religious community, and especially of those most withdrawn. In his later book, *The New Reformation?*, published in 1965, John Robinson quotes approvingly Bonhoeffer's description of a true Christian fellowship relevant to a genuinely "worldly" life as being one in which the salt is at least 95% of the time in solution. He then continues, "it is the exact opposite of the enclosed community—and this may be the equivalent of the dissolution of the monasteries in the new Reformation. Five per cent of the year may well represent the maximum that any Christian community or order engaged in the world should spend in being together as such".[2] He does not at that point in the argument specifically state that the enclosed order is redundant, but the whole discussion is loaded by his innate suspicion of other-worldliness and withdrawal.

No contemplative would deny that, in terms of *actual existence*, most people are temperamentally better suited by a life which is 95% active and only 5% withdrawn. For most of us, God clearly wills that both personal fulfilment in the truest sense and our personal contribution to the life around us should be achieved in a primarily active setting. But in terms of *significant existence* the proportion is quite wrong. The 5% must increasingly overflow into the 95% until work and life are seen *sub specie aeternitatis;* there is literally no future for a life almost entirely alienated from its basic source and destiny. It is indeed true that work is prayer and true also in one sense that a man's response to the unconditional must be an unconditional personal relationship, and that he must accept this commitment in every sphere of his existence. But, when a man gives himself to others in service and relationship, he is inevitably conditioned by what he himself is, and he will be what he is by means of the degree of his conformity to his own true end. Thus, in the here and now of life, he will both fulfil himself and serve his fellow-men by means of his own hold upon eternal life. There is no place in

Christian practice for the current vogue for self-expression quite irrespective of the quality of the self being expressed. The contemplative attitude, the permeation of the 95% by the 5%, offers some assurance that activity is being progressively conformed to the will of God.

It is in this context that we see the essential purpose of the contemplative life. If the world were wholly surrendered to God, there would be no sin, no deformation, either at individual or cosmic level. But there *is* sin and there *is* deformation. Only the disciplined adherence to God can begin to right it at the individual level, because there is no penitence without self-knowledge, and the self is only truly known in terms which include its essential as well as its experiential life. Only a Church which is clearly aware of the basic contribution of the contemplative life can hope to meet sin and deformation at the corporate level. Those called to the contemplative life embrace it because they are called by God, not because they are the elected representatives of the Church, fulfilling a certain function which the Church has deemed necessary for its own well-being. But, being so called, their function is clear. They are the 5%. Their work is to *be*, not to *do*.

From this function, this rationale, flows the detailed discipline and self-denial by which contemplatives, whether as individuals or as a corporate body, free themselves to be effective lovers of God, and therefore for that work of prayer which is impossible without discipline. Ascetic practice, so often a stumbling block in this day and age, has no inherent rationale as a work of self-culture, self-control, self-analysis, and self-mastery. But it is both the condition and the consequence of the contemplative attitude. The more profound the level at which this attitude orients the whole creature to its Creator, the more searching will become the ascetic discipline required. The pattern is inevitable, whether it be expressed in the individual or in the corporate life of a contemplative order.

The contemplative life is lived first as a life of praise, adoration, and thanksgiving to God, as a supreme expression of man's primary end, offered more and more perfectly as those who give themselves to it become open to God through increasing clarity and purity of vision. And thus, by the mere fact of the rhythm which Ruysbroeck so aptly described, it is lived for the salvation of men. It is the vocation of the Cross. As Geoffrey Curtis finely said in *Christian Spirituality Today*, it is a vocation which comes from "the knowledge and love of the Charity of God in Christ Jesus, requiring all the resources of faith, including mortification and, where possible, liturgy, study, withdrawal, silence, solitude. And its fruit is charity towards God, towards man, living, departed, and yet to be, and towards creation visible and invisible".[3]

There is no need for such a life to make a communication in the particularist terms which Charles Boxer would require. It *is* the communication, the most sacrificial communication it is possible to make. The world misreads the ascesis of contemplatives when it is seen as a progressive exercise in self-denial, requiring apparently more and more arbitrary interferences with the fully human and natural life. There are semi-pathological conditions which ape the detail of contemplative ascesis—and every director worthy of the name is aware of this—but basically the discipline is a response of love, accepted with increasing discretion and sureness of touch as one by one the material things which chain the spirit are relinquished before a greater claim.

Few are called to this life, but they are called for all; their life is not isolated from the main stream of the Church's life, but separated for their particular purpose of praise and prayer.

It is hardly surprising that in the Anglican Church the contemplative orders were a late growth. The rediscovery of the ideals and purpose of community life in the second half of the nineteenth century owed much to devoted women who struggled through all kinds of uncomprehending public criticism to enjoy at last some measure of support and approval because they were seen to be active in "good works." Many of the pioneers would not themselves have understood at that stage the essential features of a contemplative order. In any case, they would have been forced into what has been termed the "mixed life", part active and part contemplative, because any other foundation would have seemed unthinkable to the earnest public opinion of Victorian times.

The work of the mixed communities has diversified and prospered in all parts of the Anglican communion, and they show today a flexibility and degree of imagination which is enabling them to meet situations of distress and disturbance where help from other sources is still only marginal.

By the turn of the century, however, a new call of a rather different kind was making itself heard, and contemplative communities for women were founded at a time when opinion in the Church could more readily accept the notion of withdrawal primarily for the work of prayer. The late growth was a persistent growth. The seed grew secretly, but so effectively that, during the years immediately following the second world war, contemplative Orders for women often had proportionately a greater number of postulants and novices than the more active orders. Foundations for men have run into considerable difficulties, but they persist; and one day the work of men like William of Glasshampton and Robert Gofton-Salmond will be fully recognized as a vital contribution to the life of the Church.

Meanwhile, it is essential that the Orders we have should not be forced by current secularist attitudes and the logic of "worldly Christianity" into an abandonment of principle through loss of nerve. They stand on something of a razor edge. On the one hand, they are increasingly extending their contacts with the Church as a whole, as and where it may seem desirable, in order to become the well whence others may draw, a development which has naturally led to some modifications in the principles of enclosure, and perhaps to a certain degree of tension as to how far these modifications should go. On the other hand, there are signs that some are being drawn to an even more solitary or anchoretic life, and tentative provision is being made for them.

There is obviously much to be gained from the support which the contemplative communities can give to the Church and to the world at large, but it would be disastrous if this were interpreted almost as a deeper means of self-justification through a deeper level of service. If the contemplative attitude is valid, then the contemplative life is valid, and need make no concession to good works, even of so exalted a kind.

However forcefully the plea for re-integration with the world, or for salvation through this re-integration, may be expressed to members of contemplative orders, or even voiced within them, the fact remains that the contemplative religious must demonstrate par excellence that his primary integration must be with God. He must make it clear that he is specifically called to the degree of apartness and withdrawal which for him makes that integration possible. Within the solidarity of Christ's mystical body, the Church, he engages in that primary battle with evil whose mysterious strategy is largely and necessarily hidden from those on whose behalf it is waged.

If the contemplative orders are to remain true to their fundamental calling, they need the sympathy and under-standing of their fellow Christians. Most contemplative monks and nuns have experienced for themselves the truth of Christ's statement, "You have not chosen me, but I have chosen you". Acceptance of the call, however, is only the beginning of a vocation which is deeply and authentically marked by suffering to its end. One of the fiercest and most recurrent temptations is the desire to abandon the accepted commitment for paths where intelligently applied effort shows more demonstrable results; the strength of this inner temptation is today being reinforced to an almost unprece-dented extent by external pressure. It is pitiable that a Roman Catholic Carmelite friar should have to say, despite theoreti-cal appreciation of the contemplative life expressed in his Church in the highest and most authoritative places, that he and his fellows in practice "may well find themselves fighting a losing battle against the forces not of evil, but of good". So, failing to obtain sympathy even from their fellow religious of other communities, "the best they can do is to plead for immunity".[4]

In the Anglican church, where the contemplative life has a much shorter history, the damage which can be done by uncomprehending criticism is far greater. Can they also not plead for immunity, knowing that they support by prayer and sacrifice the active work of those who would have them come out to share it? Even if numerical strength alone were in question, the gain in active helpers would be negligible if every contemplative monk and nun in the Church of England came out to labour in the parishes and in industrial missions. In terms of spiritual strength, the loss would be incalculable. We must surely not incur the guilt of destroying what we have begun with such difficulty to build.

As we grow older, most of us are tempted sometimes to wonder what use we have made of time and talent. St John of the Cross, contemplative saint writing for contemplative friars and nuns, left a directive on this very matter. He did not ask them to consider whether they had finally devised a system of self-discipline which freed them from all the temptations of the world, the flesh, and the devil; he did not ask them to redouble their efforts to reach still higher levels of prayer and recollection. He merely warned them—"in the evening they will examine you in love".[5] The most contemporary theologian could ask nothing better.

6

Intercession:
Sympathetic Magic or the
Power of God?

◆

It may seem strange to leave to this stage a consideration of the relevance of the contemplative attitude to what is apparently the simplest prayer of all, the asking prayer, the first thing most of us ever learn. It is perhaps even more odd to turn to this after an apologia for the life of contemplative communities.

I choose to do this because the "simplest prayer of all" has highly problematical aspects which engage the attention of all thinking Christians from university professors to the small heterogenous groups of parishioners meeting for Lenten discussion. Wherever questions on the subject of prayer are invited, the same uncertainty and unease shows itself: "Ought we to pray for success/health/victory in war? Does God answer prayer? What effect do my prayers for other people have?" I believe that it is only in the context of the contemplative attitude, and above all of the final and total commitment of the contemplative life, that we can begin to grasp any sort of answer to the problems which meet every Christian every time he prays.

The problem is universal in the Church, and of so pressing a nature that it is often a root-cause for the abandonment by a majority of church-goers of any serious attempt to pray at all. But the solution lies at a very deep level of spiritual apprehension, and we need to be shown where to look for it by the experience of those who have staked their whole lives on the answer they have perceived—uncertainly at first, but with increasing conviction as the demands of it unfold in their own particular patterns of sacrifice and self-giving.

On the face of it, the justification of simple petitionary prayer, whether for ourselves or others, looks straightforward enough. A Christian might not unnaturally take the point of view that neither Christ nor his Church would recommend a practice fundamentally irrelevant and ineffective. When therefore both the Scriptures and the tradition of the Church approve direct "asking" prayers, he is predisposed to get on with the job as best he can. But then he reflects that scientific enquiry has demonstrated a relationship of cause and effect in the natural world which seems to leave little room for the cruder answers to prayer by means of a naive interference by the Creator in the accepted rhythms of his creation. In any case, the stark Old Testament equation of sin with punishment, of the worship of false gods with famine and invasion, seems oddly anthropomorphic even to a world which can make a dust-bowl in pursuit of greater productivity. Doubt on this point undermines confidence in much more subtle forms of petition and intercession, and the Christian is often left wondering whether there is something basically unrealistic about the entire revelation of God in Christ.

One point of fact is worth immediate notice, and that is the essential *simplicity* of the material provision prayed for in the Lord's Prayer; it is merely a request for daily bread, not a grocery list. The rest of the prayer is concerned primarily with the establishment of a right relationship with God and man. Further instruction on prayer in the Gospels— "ask and ye shall receive" and so on—needs to be understood in the light of the pattern prayer; we should then at least be delivered from the detailed directives to the Almighty which disfigure some of our public services and our panic sessions of private prayer.

On the contrary, the Gospel narratives suggest that the core of our Lord's precept and practice of prayer was "Thy will be done". To offer this as an answer to those troubled about their prayers, however, often seems a singularly cool piece of verbal sleight-of-hand. I remember some thirty years ago entering a room with an agnostic friend and seeing two framed texts, hung one above the other. The upper one read, "Ask and ye shall receive"; the lower, "Ask anything according to His will". My friend laughed, and remarked with some cynicism that this was certainly a neat way out of the difficulty. Nowadays, the unease surrounding the problem of intercessory prayer may be expressed in more sophisticated terms, but the juxtaposition of these two directives is still seen as the somewhat evasive qualification of the one by the other, instead of as the complete explanation which traditional spirituality offers.

It is significant, and entirely verifiable, that more advanced prayer is less concerned with specific requests than the prayer of children or beginners. The cynic might suggest that the negligible incidence of results has proved discouraging to the experienced, but the man who prays less specifically often gives much more time and offort to his prayers—and this doesn't look like discouragement. He is in fact less concerned to look for answers.

Again, the man who really practises prayer finds that, the more he loves the people he prays for, the less he is inclined to prescribe remedies for their troubles or prefer requests on their behalf. Depth of love for them coupled with depth of love for God makes him uncertain of his capacity to discern what is really for their good. An attitude of trust takes the place of anxiety, and already the problem of petition is less exacting. Panic prayers, on the contrary, generally exhibit both less trust and more prescription. Mathematics at university level presents problems very different from those encountered in the fourth form, but it is still a valid and recognizable development of number work, to the expert even if not to the first year man! A little higher education in the spiritual life brings torment and struggle enough, but the problems are different, and the earlier ones seem not to matter any more.

The language of trust is the language of commitment, for oneself as much as for others, and it is in this context that the why and how of petition becomes clearer. It is not in fact the beginners' prayer it may seem, since it is essentially a prayer of conformity to the will of God; and conformity is the fruit of long practice in just that contemplative experience of God which is the most searching and demanding prayer of all.

This means neither that a child's list of petitions is a waste of time, nor that the promise to pray for people is meaningless. A child will express his concern for an anxious mother by bringing her his favourite woolly animal, and the mother accepts the love and offering for what it is. We abandon a great many over-simplified attitudes as we make progress in any field of knowledge, and so it is with prayer. We start where we are; and indeed from God's point of view there may seem very little difference between the careful, loving prayer of the child and the absorbed stillness of a contemplative nun; the offering is all.

Similarly, we are right to ask for prayers and to promise to pray for others, however rudimentary we feel our spiritual experience to be; for prayer is the most practical thing imaginable. It is the invited co-operation between man's weak and ill-informed will and the will of God, and therefore an illimitable expansion of his own thin and uncomprehending charity by the charity of God, an enhancement of his own poverty-stricken power for good by a potency which is infinite and almighty.

It is perhaps worth considering a specific instance of intercessory prayer to discover how the word "practical" may be applied to it, and I hope I may be forgiven for introducing here a personal note.

Some years ago, we were faced as a family with a situation where the decisions to be made would probably have major repercussions on the rest of our lives, and we were much in need of advice and encouragement. Helpful suggestions came from several quarters; but the response of a friend of many years' standing, a busy priest heavily engaged at diocesan as well as parochial level, was a promise to get up considerably earlier each day during the crucial period to pray for "your intention in the matter"; not, be it noted, for "your desires". Mercifully, we can try to intend the will of God despite the crude clamour of the emotions.

The sacrifice of sleep was offered simply and directly as the service of a friend, and could only be accepted with equal simplicity and directness, and with humility and gratitude.

What sort of evaluation can be made of the results of this offering?

In the first place, an assurance of friendly support and sympathy, and still more of active help within a frame of reference I found wholly valid, did much to enable me to meet the situation with some degree of equanimity. It is probable too that the resulting quietness of mind materially affected the way in which the situation was handled. It is after all part of the economy of God's action to use natural channels of power and communication when they are laid open to him.

Again, it was a demonstration of Christian solidarity. Psychologists and sociologists have explored in depth this notion of the solidarity of the human race, and have demonstrated that it is far more than imaginative fiction. To put oneself wholly and peacefully at the disposal of God for the sake of friends in a state of anxiety would seem, on these grounds also, to be a not wholly unrealistic piece of service. Furthermore, however doubtful some of the results of researches into the phenomena of para-psychology may be, there does appear to be an indication that the relationship between one personality and another can be much more cogent and mysterious than we have hitherto imagined—and how much more so when the relationship is between Christians and is enclosed within a mutual relationship with God.

But the true result of this prayer offered and accepted lay at a more profound level still. The effective offering was sacrifice, taken up and enhanced, as all Christian self-denial must be, by the sacrifice of the Cross; the effective result prayed for was conformity to the will of God for all concerned in the situation, whatever the detail of its outcome. Prayer made *through* sacrifice *for* conformity is prayer which tips the balance of the scales against human frailty, obstinacy, and incomprehension. It is the secret and hidden exercise under God of power for reparation and renewal. Even incarnate God could ask the prayers of his friends. "Could you not watch with me one hour?" is an expression not of casual regret but of poignant loss.

Perhaps it now becomes easier to distinguish the correct dispositions for the prayer of petition. Clearly we cannot postpone prayer for others and for ourselves until we are assured of our own purity of intention, quite apart from the fact that the more we pray the less we like the look of our own motives. But one has to start somewhere, and a grasp of the true frame of reference will perhaps prevent us from marching confidently down all the wrong roads.

It is interesting that some contemporary theologians, having rejected the traditional attitude to the supernatural, have inevitably a "this-worldly" attitude to intercession. They are obviously happier with an expression of concern for other people through being "*with them*, in silence or compassion or action", than through being *with God*. The words quoted are John Robinson's, and he continues, "My own experience is that I am really praying for people, agonizing with God for them, precisely *as* I meet them and really give my soul to them . . . to open oneself to another *unconditionally* in love *is* to be with him in the presence of God, and that is the heart of intercession. To pray for another is to expose both oneself and him to the common ground of our being; it is to see one's concern for him in terms of *ultimate* concern, to let God into the relationship. Intercession is to *be with* another at that depth".[1] The italics in this passage are the author's, but there is an unitalicized phrase which I find profoundly significant of the slant on intercession which a "non-religious" understanding of prayer is bound to have. The phrase is— *"agonizing* with God *for them"*—and here the italics are mine.

The words have a highly-charged emotive content, and we have all come away from such agonizing sessions, whether on our knees or in personal relationship, and known ourselves drained of energy and spiritually spent. I suppose in some obscure way we take it for granted that virtue has gone out from us, and are aware that there has been a considerable element of self-giving. The crucial question asks what *sort* of self we have given and what sort of result we were expecting. Judging by the amount of agony suffered *at the time of the encounter*, our selfhood has been in a fair degree of disturbance, and our degree of involvement a concentrated energizing of all our desires and hopes for a particular person at a particular time—and quite probably for a particular result. I remember misusing an entire retreat some years ago by regarding it as an opportunity to pray almost continuously for two people in crisis-situations, and then later feeling cheated when neither situation seemed to have been resolved in a manner which gave one any confidence for the future.

It is very difficult in this state of emotional disturbance to distinguish between true self-offering and a surrender to pressures which in fact cut us off from God's action, and interpose between us and him a concentration on the person or situation we pray about which is closer to magic than to the work of the Holy Spirit. The Spirit indeed "prayeth in us with groanings which cannot be uttered", but he has no effective entry until we have cleared out the clutter of self-directed energy, and by a long process of spiritual training have learned something of the cost of *peaceful*, prayerful dependence on God.

Christian revelation shows us Christ redeeming the world not by his miracles of healing or provision for the weary, not even by his inspiring presence and preaching, but by the final act of self-offering on the Cross. There his silence was in marked contrast both to the aggressive and hostile chatter of his enemies and to the emotional despair of most of his supporters. But, being lifted up, as he himself said, he drew, and still draws, all men to him; and true intercession will draw the world to God because it is rooted by his grace in conformity to his Cross.

The developed prayer of petition then will be humble, dependent, peaceful, and sacrificial, and the energy in it will be the energy of God, not of ourselves. Some of us may object on grounds of churchmanship to the wording—or even the idea—of saying or hearing Mass for other people, but it is a very handy piece of shorthand in the field of religious language. It makes it perfectly clear that we pray in Christ and through Christ, and that our offering is worthless unless we are prepared to stand where he stood: and it will take most of us a lifetime and more to get there. There will be agonizing in every such journey, but it will be hidden, and very rarely indeed related to the actual time of encounter with others, whether in prayer or in action. It will in fact be the agony of the whole contemplative vocation, from the first stirrings which *must* inform the prayer of all who take God seriously to the extraordinarily fruitful prayer of the saint, charged with an effectual power which occasionally breaks clean through the clumsy modes of human communication.

The lives of the saints, in fact, even when we discount hagiographical embroidery, provide numerous examples of the mysterious interplay which develops between personalities when prayer is offered by one to whom the Holy Spirit has almost unrestricted entry. We hear and read of these occasions, and are bewildered or inspired roughly in ratio to our own grasp at least of the principles of the operation. There was St Catherine of Siena's vociferous opponent, Father Lazzarino, who hoped to see for himself that all his attacks upon her integrity were justified, and, as a result of her prayer for him, was dramatically introduced to his own shortcomings. St Teresa exercised a real ministry of reconciliation through her prayer, and, in our own day, Evelyn Underhill, writing of the priestly vocation, unwittingly revealed her own—"he is meant to be one of the channels by and through which the Eternal God, manifested in time, acts within the human world, reaches out, seeks, touches, and transforms human souls".[2]

But I would like finally to quote from accounts of two holy Orthodox monks, whose lives significantly expressed both the cost and the manner of true intercession.

In 1945 there was published Julia de Beausobre's extra-ordinarily evocative treatment of the legend of Serafim of Sarov, a Russian monk who died in 1833. The story as she tells it, founded partly on the official biographies, partly on floating tradition, is illumined by her own insight and sensiti-vity. She has thus given us a most moving and profound des-cription of a man whose painful and solitary path to God led him to perceive God's purpose for hundreds of his fellow-men, and by prayer to free them to fulfil it. When he returned from the forests to become a spiritual director, a "staretz", he never closed his door to those whose need was greatest. But what they took away with them was neither a specific answer to their problems nor careful instruction in the ways of the spiritual life. "He neither spoke to his visitors nor looked at them, but, standing before the ikons, listened carefully to what they said. When he knelt down and *ceased to be con-scious of their presense*, they went away". Almost invariably they found that their lives acquired a new direction, while he, the well from which they had drawn wisdom and insight, drank from the one source that could replenish him—"and every day, after the communion of contemplation, his love and endurance were greater than the demand".[3]

The other account reveals a little more explicitly the spiritual processes here at work. Archbishop Anthony Bloom quotes from the life of the staretz Silouan, a Russian peasant who became a monk at Mount Athos in 1892, and died as re-cently as 1938. He was asked why the workers in his charge were always efficient, joyful, and creative despite the fact that they were unsupervised. The answer needs to be quoted

in full, for it takes us to the heights of contemplative intercession.

"The staretz said that he went to his cell and began to pray
for each of the workers, for their every need. To begin with,
he recalled that he was so full of concern and compassion
that he remembered nothing but them. But gradually as he
was interceding before God, praying for them with all his
being, he became more aware of the growing presence of God.
At a certain moment, he could no longer remember the earth
because the Lords presence had become so tangible and intense that he forgot all things but God. He continued praying,
going deeper and deeper into this divine presence, until at the
core of it he found the divine love concerned with the very
people he had left behind. Having forgotten them because he
could only remember the Lord, he was seized by the divine
love and brought back to earth. The divine love had taken
flesh and become man, to pray again, to intercede, but with
new strength, depth and completeness, not only as fellow-
man, but as fellow-man in whom the Spirit speaks".

There is perhaps one further point which needs to be made.
Often, the prayer of agonized concern concentrated upon a
particular person or situation is likely to be a dangerous and
disturbing piece of self-projection rather than an extension
of the peace and power of God. But there are occasions when
the prayer of contemplation, whether joyful or arid, is invaded by the apparently irresistible compulsion to draw someone by prayer into the purpose and will of God. Psychologists
may explain this by a sudden uprush from the subconscious,
but one has known of cases where the compulsion has been
curiously linked with a critical situation of which nothing
was known at the time. Some would place these incidents
firmly in the realm of extra-sensory perception—and so they
may be; but when they happen to men deeply committed to
the life of prayer, there is surely more than a suspicion that
here was a call to redemptive work, especially as the experience has nothing whatsoever in common with the anxious
and agonized strivings into which we so easily plunge.

We have come to a realm where spiritual experience can only be verified by spiritual apprehension, and a long way from the discussion of "answers to prayers" and the "value of intercession". But I would insist that we are not in some strange and exotic region, but have come by a recognizable route, even if for the final stages we have only the fragmentary maps made by those who have gone ahead of us. For them, as for us, the inspiration of the journey is God, and the way the strait way of the imitation of Christ; there is no by-pass.

7

New and Traditional
Spirituality

FAILURE OF COMMUNICATION?

The contemplative attitude is clearly a valid approach to a religion of revelation. The developed principles of Christian life which spring from it cohere into a relevant and self-consistent system of spiritual theology. Our spiritual life is necessarily rooted in our doctrinal outlook; it is as we contemplate the historic revelation of God in Christ that we learn how to conform ourselves to Christ in the world. We are never spiritual on our own or by the light of nature; we learn our spirituality within the tradition of the Church and by the light of grace.

The most insidious criticism of this approach, widely canvassed at the present time, leads not to outright condemnation, but to the suggestion that for many people this "biblical-historical-theological-orthodox tradition" no longer has power to shape their lives.[1] There must therefore be two very different modes of spirituality. On the one hand, there is traditional spirituality with all its apparatus of rules of life, times for withdrawal, methods of prayer, and patterns of discipline and self-denial. But, since this is apparently no longer helpful and meaningful to a large majority of Christians, there is also a new way. Just as we have a new theology and a new morality at this present time, so we are moving towards a new spirituality, with new structures more in tune with the contemporary scene and therefore correctly termed secular spirituality. We are invited to regard this latter as more appropriate to a period when the patterns of religious behaviour which hold God and man in relationship are in process of radical change.

It seems churlish, when we are told that "the old ways will probably continue for many for ever",[2] to cast doubts upon the adequacy of the new way. But is the new way any more in fact than an adulterated version of the old, an attempt perhaps to understress fundamentals in order to lay a somewhat isolated emphasis on patterns of living which, however genuinely Christian, are derivative? Traditional spirituality is a system of far greater profundity, relevance, and flexibility than many Protestant theologians are prepared to admit. For far too long Protestant comment has centred more upon the accidents of traditional spiritual growth than on its substance. It has tended to get out of proportion the more spectacular aspects of this growth, contrasting it first with the sober Biblical piety of reformed religion and latterly with the holy worldliness of the "new Reformation".

In fact the names of the great saints and doctors of the Church rarely appear in the works of the new theologians. If they are mentioned at all they are frequently misunderstood because they have not been sufficiently seriously studied.

And yet Professor Tinsley can write, "The Christian mystics, in the place they give to the imitation of Christ, had the same aim as modern existentialists: to relate the past events of the historical Jesus to the present life of the believer. In the long run, in spite of its excesses, mysticism turns out to be more deeply rooted in the historical revelation in Christ than many of its critics allow—and the necessary polarity in the Christian life between the facts of Christ and the work of the Spirit has never been better expressed than by an undoubted mystic, St Bernard of Clairvaux".[3] We neglect at our peril the practical experience of those who have authentically been "friends of God", and confine ourselves to our very great loss within the circumscribed climate of the last fifty, or even ten, years.

There is certainly evidence enough that Christians of all types are finding their "interior life" profoundly unsatisfactory, and they are obviously and rightly predisposed to look for any new insights which may offer solutions to their problems. In his editorial preface to *Spirituality for Today* Eric James refers to his extensive contacts with the parochial clergy and says that he "cannot doubt that the traditional forms of spirituality have gone dead on many of the most conscientious clergy, who are often discouraged, perplexed, guilty, even shocked at what has befallen them". The very terms in which he describes their state lead one to suppose that many of them could be helped not by less traditional spirituality, but by more. He is describing in recognizable terms a recognizable state, for which there are recognizable remedies. Dean Coburn gives a similar account of the state of young clergy and ordinands in America, but here apparently the traditional methods have been discarded even earlier in adult life as unsuitable, or even harmful.

Two comments need to be made here. In the first place, a great many people discard the traditional practices of spirituality before they have ever seriously tried them, bringing to their use far less patience and disciplined attention than they would expect to bring to almost any other activity in which they hope to make progress, be it discus-throwing or nuclear physics. A student of theology who expects to give five minutes of his day to private prayer is not really trying it out; however actively he may engage in intellectual debate or social service, he is not qualified to pronounce on the efficacy of the traditional ways of spiritual life. Some theological colleges, in this country at any rate, still expect to guide their students to a more time-consuming pattern of prayer, but here we come up against the second point—the lack of expert knowledge and the rooted distrust of expertise in the ways of spiritual theology.

Within the Church of England the notion has persisted for far too long that, in this particular pastoral situation, loving concern and attention to duty make priestcraft, in the sense of a sound knowledge of spiritual theology, not only unnecessary but suspect. The very word is loaded, despite the fact that it means no more than the professional skill of the priest.

Over the last ten years of so much has clearly been done to extend the range of professional training in theological colleges. Ordinands are given wide opportunities of specialized training in fields most suited to them, in techniques of teaching, pastoral counselling, the spiritual care of the mentally handicapped, and so on.

But the spiritual training of the future priest is of paramount importance; and still he does not always find that he has easy access, during his years of preparation, to those who can guide him in this field from profound knowledge and costly personal experience. The report *Theological Colleges for Tomorrow* rightly stresses that "crises of personal faith and commitment are apt to be a perennial experience for those who enter the sacred ministry".[4] It tends, however, to see a more apposite remedy for this in the use of critical reasoning, exposure to "questioning", than in laying a sound foundation of knowledge in that field of theology which used to be called ascetic and mystical theology and now is more properly termed spiritual theology. Disciplined training in the life of prayer needs to go hand in hand with expert instruction in spiritual theology if faith and practice are to be seen to cohere. And in this context it must be remembered that the Church of England is catholic as well as reformed, and not only may, but should, draw upon the resources of the Roman and Orthodox Churches as well as on those of continental protestantism.

There are fortunately theological colleges where much care and thought is given to this aspect of training, but the comparative youth and inexperience of a distinct proportion of the staffs of these colleges present an obvious limitation to the amount of help which can be given in this field, however valuable a contribution may be made elsewhere. It would appear that mistakes and misjudgements are still too often made. I would instance the case of an ordinand of considerable intellectual calibre who was told even by a senior member of staff that there should always be much "intellectual content" in his prayers, because he would otherwise find his prayer-life thin and unsuited to his mental capacity. This would seem to represent an elementary mistake in spiritual direction, and it is hardly surprising that much frustration and misery followed.

For anyone, priest, layman or laywoman, in fact, the discovery of wise and informed guidance is more a matter of luck than it should be.

In the past many have relied upon the practice of Retreat to put them in touch with the right sort of help, but nowadays there is no guarantee that retreat-conductors themselves will not have abandoned the more traditional outlook. Some disquieting things are being said in retreat houses, and to people with insufficient knowledge of the current theological debate to see the remarks in context. A busy housewife, for instance, often has to make complicated arrangements to fit in even one short weekend retreat in a year, and relies upon husband and friends to make it possible. She is not helped (and I quote from personal knowledge) by being asked what "non-religious" activities she chooses to engage in, since these are "the real test of her Christian commitment". For the woman in question non-religious activities needed no choosing! But the making of a retreat, especially for the first time, often involves hesitation and anxiety. A wife and mother is all too easily made to feel guilty if she has relied on others to make her brief withdrawal possible. There is a place for challenge and a place for brash debating points, and a wise guide knows the difference.

There is more than a little evidence in any case that the practice of retreat, a very typical exercise in the field of traditional spirituality, is being undermined by a basic misconception of its purpose. And this is doubly unfortunate be-

cause the Anglican contribuion to the theory and practice of
retreat has been quite distinctive. Building upon the rather
different practice characteristic of western catholicism as a
whole, our own Church has developed methods which Rome
herself is studying with interest and appreciation.

But now it is not only Dean Coburn who suggests that
retreats should no longer be conducted in silence "where the
only voice is the voice of the conductor, the 'specialist' in
holy matters", but should provide opportunities for "sharing
and dialogue".[5] A warden of a retreat house, writing in July
1967 to the President of the Association for Promoting Retreats, referred to a growing tendency to reduce the silence
to a minimum and to turn parochial retreats, already necessarily short, into a mixture of conference and retreat.

In his annual report, the President rightly emphasized that
"silence is a primary necessity for a sustained effort to realize
the presence of God and to hold uninterrupted converse with
him".[6] A well-instructed retreatant goes into retreat not to
listen to a set of addresses, the voice of the "specialist in holy
matters", but to give attention, in a silence which can rarely
be secured in the normal way of life, to the overriding claims
of God upon his personality and his life. By means of a true
retreat we should be able to move out of the area of debate
and dialogue into the wholesome and enlightening climate of
God. The addresses may or may not be helpful, but in any
case they are preparatory rather than primarily instructive.
The real work of the retreat is done elsewhere, and those
who most value and understand the practice of retreat are
least likely to welcome the invasion of their silence by yet
more "meaningful discussion". Some in fact now make preliminary enquiries on just this point!

We are rightly anxious to introduce to the practice of
retreat people who may find the whole idea daunting. But
silence is the most distinctive quality of retreat, and never
more needed than at the present time. It would be a great
loss if, in our anxiety to woo the doubtful by a proliferation
of "retreat-conferences", we crowded out the true retreat.

Surprisingly, the newcomer to the practice often looks back
with considerable appreciation to a first experience of uninterrupted quiet. He may in fact be keener to repeat the
process than if he had attended yet another conference with
a few silent periods. I remember a coach-load of youngsters
from a tough Midland parish who were so impressed by their
first genuinely quiet weekend that they sat in relaxed, de-
lighted, but total silence all the way home! At the next youth
club meeting they asked how soon they could go again.

The failure of some exponents of new spirituality to appreciate the silence of retreat seems to be symptomatic of a gap
in communication over a much wider field. We have already
seen that the theologians who share the *Honest to God* outlook tend to minimize the importance of the supernatural
element in the Christian faith. Inevitably, therefore, they
approach the writings of traditional spirituality, if they read
them at all, with a marked distrust of the "otherworldly" and
therefore "unrealistic" emphases they think they find there.

"I am convinced", writes Eric James, "that spirituality must
be related to men in their actual decisions, actions (and inability and incapacity to decide and act), their involvement
in human affairs—domestic, commercial, industrial, civic,
professional, national, and so on. If someone then says (as I
am sure they will!), 'Ah, but spirituality is to do with being
more than doing', I would say, 'Yes, but it has to do with
existential being, which cannot nicely be separated from
doing and acting' ".[7] He would contend, therefore, that the
stuff of life as it is lived provides true spirituality, for all life
is spiritual. God is in the world and that is where he is to be
served and found. It is in involvement with the world that a
man's authentic self, and therefore his true integrity, will be
developed.

But is there not here a confusion between two aspects of
the world? There must surely be a distinction between the
world as God's creation, the object of his love, the stuff of
existence with which we make contact from our first sentient
acts and responses, and the world estranged from God by its

rebellious rejection of his purposes for it. Involvement must therefore be balanced by a kind of detachment which enables us to live *in* the world in the first sense, but to be not *of* the world in the second sense.

In a series of addresses based on the Spiritual Exercises of St Ignatius, Karl Rahner quotes the saint, "The other things on the face of the earth are created for man, to help him in attaining the end for which he is created", and then most lucidly comments on the implications for contemporary theology—"I should realize that nothing can take the place of my pure ego, that I cannot run away from it, that I cannot relinquish my self-responsibility to the world around me". Man must in fact learn how to separate himself from the "other things" as part of the road to sanctity, so that the "free self-surrendering person posited by God" can see them as the situation of his service and worship, but, while still having a positive relationship to the things of creation, can grasp the nature of sin as "the disturbance of the objective order of things", and can learn to take or leave them, to use them as they were meant to be used, and direct all his dealings with them towards God.[8]

This profound and thoroughly orthodox understanding of detachment and involvement has nothing in common with unconcern. But equally it can have little in common with certain current expositions of situation ethics. Man may be modern man, scientific man, armed with his empirical methods and his principles of scientific verification, but he is still the child of God; and, as T. R. Miles remarks in his book *Religion and the Scientific Outlook*, "sentences containing the word God cannot normally be regarded as quasi-scientific explanations of empirically discovered events".[9]

The continuing significance of personal choice is, therefore, even more obvious to the orthodox spiritual theologian than to the existentialist philosopher. But we make our choices in accordance with the kind of people we are and, by virtue of the examined life, may hope to become. We are only authentically man, fully human, as we are set free, by conformity

with Christ, to fulfil our authentic purpose to be a child of
God.

The rule of life, and all that is thus implied of spiritual
training and discipline, is simply the imitation of Christ. In
seeking to make it and live by it, we are in no sense erecting
a system and calling it God. We are recognizing that our
religion is incarnational, that the body functions in an orderly
and rhythmical manner, and that habit, far from being a
repressive strait-jacket, is, if properly formed and fostered,
a very important aid to the redemption of the body.

Habits of discipline and devotion gradually form in us the
disposition to go on seeking to know and do the truth when
enthusiasm ebbs, when the insidious tug of selfishness is more
than usually hard to resist and, worst of all, when the "noon-
day devil", the familiar spirit of many a middle-aged parish
priest, attacks the very ground of his faith.

As with modes of discipline, so with methods of prayer.
The method is not something which has a validity in itself.
It is wholly related to the aim of prayer and, if we see it out
of that context, we shall certainly draw wrong conclusions.
Every branch of secular knowledge is deeply concerned at
this present time with learning techniques; the knowledge of
God's purposes, and of our own reactions to them, imparted
by prayer similarly requires the patient and intelligent use
of all our resources and the willingness to listen to the
experience of experts in the field.

There is an element of sheer misunderstanding about the
current conviction that the teaching of traditional spirituality
on the life of prayer is inflexible and didactic in approach.
Again and again the really great masters of prayer insist that
no two people pray alike. "God leads each soul along different
roads", says St John of the Cross, "and there shall hardly be
found a single spirit who can walk even half the way which
is suitable for another".[10] Nearer to our own day, Père Grou,
for all his apparent strictness and austerity, offers the same
gentle and wise advice. "Do not use so many books and exer-
cizes and methods. Let your heart tell you what you wish to

say to God. He does not want so much formality in his service; great harm has ben done by the reduction of devotion to a fine art dependent on so many rules".[11]

It is in fact the secondary and much less inspired authors who have so often falsified the teaching of the masters, and have developed distinctions and degrees which are foreign to the insight and perception of the original.

Nevertheless the door is not thus left open to rampant individualism and ill-disciplined self-expression in either prayer or activity. Despite the variety in detail in authentic patterns of Christian prayer and discipline, there is an underlying unity of approach. The end proposed is the same, the way is the same, the straight and narrow way of the imitation of Christ; and human psychology varies less over the centuries than we are inclined to believe.

The great masters may be impatient of rigid rules, but of the necessity of rule in the sense of ordered discipline they have not the slightest doubt. The basis of all forms of renunciation is love, just as love will inspire and direct the greatest renunciation of all, that which presents itself daily in the unselfregarding practice of the duties of our state and the service of others, wherever God chooses we should be.

Ascetic discipline is first and foremost a positive expression of that love, a positive search for the means of purity of heart and intention. Its more restrictive aspect is simply the overflow of love seeking to control self-will and self-concern. Every true authority in the spiritual life makes it clear that self-regarding pietism pursued at the expense of one's fellowmen is a puny and limited exercise pursued at the expense of our love of God. But any such authority is equally clear that the training of the will is a long and arduous process which cannot be by-passed by the most ardent lover of his fellow-men.

"Anyone who is truly reformed to God's likeness", says our own very English master, Walter Hilton, of Thurgarton in Nottinghamshire, "must *devote much effort* to keeping this likeness whole and pure, so that it does not degenerate into the image of sin through weakness of will". How much more will this be the case when, as with most of us, reformation to God's likeness lies very far in the future. "No one", continues Walter Hilton, "can leap from the lowest rung of the ladder and land on the top. He must mount each rung in succession; and so it is in the spiritual life. No one is suddenly endowed with all graces, but when God, the source of all grace, helps and teaches a soul, it can attain this state by sustained spiritual exercises and wisely ordered activity".[12] And yet even here this uncompromising teaching coexists with a gentle and discerning warning against ill-considered zeal and anxious scrupulosity.

The general temper of the real expert in the matter is wise, spacious, and refreshingly free of preconceived notions. It is easy enough to take individual directives, addressed to a particular person, of particular temperament, at a particular stage in history and, by presenting them out of context, demonstrate their unsuitability as a guide-book for modern man. But an individual route-map produced on request by the Automobile Association is not a vade-mecum for every traveller. The stark negations of St John of the Cross, the intimate self-revelations of St Teresa of Avila, the austerities of St Serafim of Sarov, the narrow and circumscribed life of the exiled Père Grou—all these are easily misunderstood and caricatured. But their writings, and those of many others who have asked much of themselves and much of those who sought their advice in trying to live the life of prayer, together offer an impressive body of evidence that the ascent of the human spirit to God, and the processes of learning the life of love, Godward and manward, follow broadly similar lines.

Far from being out of touch, eccentric, and vaguely theatrical, they all have something to say to us which is immensely relevant; but we need to remember that it is something to which we are constitutionally ill-disposed to listen. We have the same trouble when we read the Gospels and are apt to take refuge in theories about the language of hyperbole and the evidence of later accretions. We shall naturally therefore welcome an alternative way of spirituality, especially if it offers an apparent emancipation from detailed and persistent endeavour in largely hidden fields and projects us instead into modes of activity which may flatter our public and private image. The fully-integrated, wholly authentic Christian is a saint—and the saint notoriously gets a bad contemporary press.

"NEW" CONTEMPLATION

There is, however, one aspect of the new spirituality which appears to offer a direct challenge to traditional teaching, the more so because it has significant links with it. I refer to the suggestion that contemplative prayer itself, with its accompanying insights, is not necessarily the fruit of a long and arduous process of spiritual training.

Dean Coburn states the case persuasively. "It seems to be a nearly universal contemporary experience that contemplation is not necessarily an advanced step in prayer which follows after a rigorous disciplined life of vocal and then mental prayer, but may indeed be a form of prayer which even a beginner (howbeit unknowingly) may embark upon. In other words, what has traditionally been thought of as a preliminary apparatus for advanced prayer is not necessarily so. It may be—at least for some—quite possible to avoid the traditional ways, and to enter more immediately upon a prayer of intent alone where there is an easy natural response to God in the midst of the daily routine". He further develops this point of view by saying that contemplation should be the "enfolding mood", and that the "self-conscious desire to dissect" the experience of prayer should be left aside. Simplicity in approach will thus by-pass artificial structures and get to the heart of things by a "direct, straightforward, simple attention to God in prayer".[13]

An interesting comment on this statement by a theologian is provided by the current preoccupation with a sanctity without God, sought by recourse to oriental traditions of self-training in awareness and concentration—a phenomenon to which reference has already been made and with which in fact radical theologians have little sympathy. As Professor Tinsley remarks, they tend to class it with the gnostic distaste for the actualities of historical and bodily existence which is typical of a false mysticism.[14] They are less ready to seek a possible explanation in an incoherent flight both from the busy activism of modern life and from current religious practices which do little to preserve any sense of the numinous.

But is this "simple prayer of intent" available to a beginner, offering him a straightforward way of attention to God? If so, does it remain essentially the prayer of a beginner? Does it point the way to a simply acquired contemplative experience which can satisfy both modern churchmen and the uncommitted in search of their inner identity?

It is worth looking fairly carefully at certain phrases Dean Coburn uses.

He first asserts that it is an almost universal contemporary experience that contemplation is a state if prayer which "even a beginner may *embark* upon", though perhaps unwittingly. Spiritual theology would say rather that it is a prayer which the beginner may *happen* upon very early in his experience of prayer. The classical authors are all well aware of the phenomenon, which they sometimes denote by the word "sweetness", a term which does not mean in this context a rather sentimental and emotional experience. "I do not deny", says Walter Hilton, "that by the grace of God a man may sometimes have some foretaste and limited experience of contemplation, for some have been granted this arly in thir spiritual life, *but they cannot retain it permanently*".[15] This sweetness or foretaste or limited experience of contemplation refers to a cessation of particular acts or forms of words in prayer accompanied by a rewarding sense of heightened awareness, not only of God, but of one's environment and the people who move in it.

People of certain temperaments have frequent experiences of this kind at the beginning of their conscious devotional life. It is allied with the experiences of nature mystics, and of all young people who have ever been transported out of themselves by a sudden intuitive sense of reality and unity with creation. They seem to represent an early state in the fight through growing consciousness of personal identity to a balanced and more abiding maturity of conception and purpose.

In prayer this state is perhaps more readily reached and appreciated in an age full-fed with verbiage, which has therefore a natural tendency to seek relief from verbal or even mental forms.

But this contemplative experience of the beginner generally differs wholly from the contemplative *state* in prayer, which implies a settled orientation away from self and towards God. Certainly the true contemplative knows that he is a beginner still, and so would agree with Coburn that contemplative prayer is not necessarily an advanced state, but his understanding of advancement will be rather different from the sense used in the quotation.

Grou sums up the situation admirably when he says it is a delusion to expect to be with the Holy Spirit in prayer and have the rest of life to oneself.[16] Fidelity and recollection are the essential prerequisites of settled contemplative prayer. If we look at the directive "let contemplation be the enfolding mood", we can perhaps not unreasonably feel suspicious of the word "mood" in this context. The advice fails lamentably when the feel of God deserts us, and the contemplative mood gives place to the long dark of aridity.

Even if we consider this "enfolding contemplative mood" as deriving authenticity from the action which it precedes or follows, we find that the traditional writers, while fully aware of the importance of the prayer of action, will not allow it to be the authenticating mode of the prayer of contemplation. Grou again is very clear. "There is a kind of prayer which is rightly named the prayer of action. Every action performed in the sight of God because it is the will of God and in the manner God wills is a prayer, and a better prayer than could be made in words at such times. All labours of body and mind unite us more closely to God. We are always praying when we are doing our duty and turning it into work for God". But this is not an endorsement of the attitude of some contemporary theologians, who tend to see withdrawal at most as part of a normal physical rhythm, and the contemplative activity as finding its true context in action—a derivation therefore rather than an affirmation. Grou, on the contrary, completes his discussion of the prayer of action by alluding to the ceaseless prayer which must underlie it; and this he defines as "a special disposition of the heart inclining it always to God".[17]

The "contemplation" then of theologians who understand it either as the prayer of the beginner, presupposing no advanced techniques, or as the prelude or postlude to action, is not the same thing as the developed and settled state described so often in the writings of spiritual theologians. The contemplative attitude may indeed lead to the developed prayer of contemplation, but only if the intention is primarily Godward and the accompanying disposition one of humble and progressive self-discpiline.

Look too at Dean Coburn's advocacy of a "direct, straightforward, simple attention to God in prayer", his insistence that we can break through artificial structures in order "not to do anything other than pray". Simplicity does not come as easily as that, as T. S. Eliot knew—"a condition of complete simplicity, costing not less than everything . . ."[18] Nowhere are the motions of our ill-disciplined desires more obvious than when we try to pray. The butterfly-like and wholly irrelevant type of distraction may indeed coexist with a very developed type of contemplative awareness, but for some of us our distractions are all too relevant, springing directly from our own divided purposes. The would-be simple, easy attention is invaded by every disorientation of the heart and mind. Mostly, when we attempt to "get to the heart of things" in prayer, it is our own heart we arrive at; and we cannot too readily dismiss Jeremiah's diagnosis—"the heart is deceitful above all things and desperately sick".

It would seem possible therefore that some contemporary theologians, in asserting that nowadays contemplation can be reached without recourse to artificial structures, are confusing discipline of *method* and discipline of *mind*. On the subject of method, the real masters are flexible and quite undoctrinaire. Where discipline of will is concerned they are inflexible, authoritative, and as uncompromising as their own Master. The discipline of will, since we are normal people operating in a physical world with physical attributes, will necessarily involve a methodical attack on disorientations, and method here means both habit and conscious purpose.

Certainly Dean Coburn is right in stressing that self-conscious dissection must be avoided. *All* the spiritual masters would agree here. Fifteen hundred years ago the monk Cassian asserted that the man who is conscious of praying is not praying at all. One feels he would have expressed even stronger condemnation of the man who self-consciously dissects his experience of prayer. But there is nothing inherently self-conscious about a right use of method which facilitates the establishment of good and useful habits of prayer.

Habit tends to be decried in some circles, especially in those influenced by existentialism, as a methodological structure which obscures natural and spontaneous response. But most of us rely on a high degree of habit formation to make sense of our daily lives, and it is by no means out of place in bringing coherence and persistence into our spiritual lives. Oddly enough, those who distrust rules of life, spiritual disciplines, and the tried methods of detachment are, in their very efforts to be this-worldly, uprooting man from his naturel environment of rhythm and regularity: and thus would seem to lay themselves open to a distrust of some of the profounder aspects of an incarnational revelation.

It would not necessarily seem then that the prevalence and popularity of some more contemplative modes of prayer, in the sense in which Dean Coburn describes the phenomenon, represent any real break-through from traditional to a new and splendidly contemporary spirituality. The analysis of the

phenomenon would seem to be amply taken care of in the
writings of the traditionalists; and they on the whole seem to
have surer remedies for the spiritual malaise which still
afflicts and discourages even those who have shouldered aside
the shackles of an apparently outworn spiritual theology.

Many a print-weary, noise-weary Christian will nowadays
instinctively turn to a quieter, less discursive form of prayer.
Moreover, debate and argument on matters of doctrine and
morals assail him so persistently through every medium of
communication that he may well feel he has all the materials
for meditation close at hand, beating in fact upon his consciousness, rather than waiting upon any systematic exercise
of memory and imagination. But this is still only the
threshold of prayer. The real heart of the matter is still conformity, and here the new spirituality does not seem to have
anything specifically new to say.

Worldly spirituality rightly finds wanting an inward-turned,
pietistic devotional life, but so would a soundly-based traditional spirituality. It rightly welcomes directness and simple
attention to God in prayer, but is surely wrong in thinking
that this can, save very exceptionally, issue from absorption
in compassionate action without any practice of the habits
and disciplines by which that simple attention is gradually
secured and maintained.

One feels there must in due course be a rehabilitation of
traditional spirituality, within which the insights and emphases of the new spirituality will find a valuable place.

Meanwhile, careful and closer study of the treasures we
have inherited would underline the essential integrity and
relevance, the balanced blend of detachment and concern inherent in the great corpus of spiritual theology. It will be for
contemporary theology, with its sociological insights, to explore the circumstances and *milieux* where the disciplined
and discerning Christian must make his specific contribution.

But the distinction between man as God's creation and man
as a fallen creature remains basic, indispensable to a Christian
understanding of man. Only a Godward-turned spirituality,

rooted and grounded in the contemplative attitude and nourished by a constant, conscious, and costly training of personality and will, can safely make that distinction.

8

Some Artistic Analogies

Contemplative experience shares no common language with modern scientific attitudes. It claims to be in touch with an Absolute which differs categorically from any finite, derivative, dependent, or contingent object.

A human being contemplating God is thus drawn into a relationship which is unique. No other relationships between finite and created objects and beings can be like the relationship between the created and the Uncreated, though the former in fact derive their validity and reality from the latter. For the contemplative all the facets of his own existence, as he grasps them in succession and delimits them one against the other, using all the techniques of argument and demonstration available to him, are yet contained within a reality which is ineffable, beyond the bounds of normal logic or communication.

This relationship will therefore be not only unique, but basically incommunicable, nor can its truth be validated by means which would be appropriate to the truths of science.

The contemplative thus appears to be at a decided disadvantage in a world conditioned by scientific and technological considerations, and in which philosophy itself, in this country at any rate, is almost exclusively empiricist in outlook. His method is intuitional rather than empiricist, he perceives what he cannot understand, experiences what he cannot investigate, and the end term of the whole process is a person rather than a proposition. To a greater or a lesser degree, he "knows". He himself is aware that the extent of his knowledge is chiefly threatened by his innate pride, but he is often somewhat surprised to be regarded by the outside world not only as a fool, but as an arrogant fool.

Even within the framework of logic, however, he could, if he wished, make out a case for himself. He is concerned to discover what he sees as the true facts of existence. Some of his pragmatically-minded critics limit fact to that which is empirically observable, and truth therefore to those facts which are verifiable within that frame of reference. But there are more aspects to an individual human being and to the universe at large than those which emerge from scientific formulation. Value judgements, for example, are of a different order and require another kind of assessment. The theologian has his own theological frame of reference. Answers to questions about the ultimate nature and meaning of the universe are given by him *within that frame of reference*, just as questions about the basic matter of the universe are answered within the physicist's frame of reference.

It would seem then that, even on logical grounds, a theological "truth" could be different in kind from a scientific "truth". For an artist, a musician, or a poet, "truth" will mean something different again, but something which will be valid within its own context of experience. Stephen Spender is not talking romantic nonsense when he says, of the creative poetic experience, "literature becomes a humble exercise of faith in being all that one can be in one's art, in being more than oneself, expecting little but with a faith in the mystery of poetry which gradually expands into a faith in the mysterious service of truth".[1] Mysterious, yes, but still truth—for him and for all engaged in the production and appreciation of artistic work.

Though scientific enquiry must have its own exacting standards of truth, some of the greatest scientists are themselves aware that the truth they offer is not the whole truth about existence. J. W. N. Sullivan, who has been described as one of the world's most brilliant interpreters of physics to the common man, puts the matter frankly—"the value of the scientist's example to the rest of mankind is limited by the fact that, in his work, the scientific man is not completely a man".[2]

In other words science gives us but a partial knowledge even of human reality, acquainting us mainly with the quantitative aspects of material phenomena. Vast areas of human experience lie right outside the field of scientific formulation. Indeed even the processes of the scientist's own creative insight are beyond the range of purely conscious calculation.

It is therefore probable that, in turning to what is loosely termed the artistic field, we may find illuminating analogies to the contemplative experience we have been considering. The search for analogies is made easier by the fact that much has recently been written about the processes and aims of the artistic imagination. It is interesting that men whose work is most clearly contemporary have often been the most fluent in exploring the processes of their own inspiration. If we find these analogies suggestive, it will perhaps therefore be doubly encouraging to contemplatives who are so often criticized for clinging to outworn attitudes.

THE AESTHETIC ATTITUDE

Creative artists themselves, and many of the critics who study their works, are in no doubt that the aesthetic attitude, differing from but not necessarily in competition with the scientific attitude, can be described in valid terms.

"It is an attitude of pure disinterested attention, partly to be defined by negation. Thus it lacks both curiosity and practical interest: it does not seek either explanations or advantages, whether the latter be selfish or otherwise. It rests delightedly in its object, which seems to gather a sometimes startling beauty and significance, and it has no ulterior end in view: It does not propose to itself either action or knowledge".[3] This quotation from a writer on poetics could describe equally well the fruitful repose which precedes the sometimes most unquiet act of artistic creation and the responsive awareness which enable eye and ear to take in, and the whole personality to assimilate, what the artist in any field is trying to express.

The remarkable thing is that it would also describe contemplative awareness in the religious sense. Both the language and the concepts could have been lifted bodily from the works of half a dozen or more spiritual writers ranging in date over hundreds of years.

There is, however, nothing really surprising in this. The author himself, pointing out that he is here describing "the aesthetic attitude at its well-developed stage",[4] goes on in fact to equate it with the contemplative attitude as pre-eminently objective. Though it can never be anything but intermittent in its ideal purity, he sees it as of its very nature emptied of self, a mature disinterested consciousness undistracted either by practical considerations or by speculative activity.

This is not to suggest that either aesthetic or contemplative experience implies a hazy, twilit state, an opting out from clear conceptual knowledge or experience in favour of a senseless and nerveless emotionalism. We have already seen that there is nothing sentimental about the contemplative attitude. It is equally the case that a high degree of intellectual awareness and a sensitivity to all levels of experience is a *sine qua non* of all really great creative activity, though the awareness and experience may be stored and absorbed at very deep levels before they begin to influence the processes of creation.

The quality of this inner life is unmistakeable to those who share it; they are likewise convinced that it differs in kind from practical life. Bradley, in his Oxford Lectures on Poetry, speaks for them all when he asserts that it is the nature of poetry "to be a world by itself, a world in which you ignore for the time being the particular conditions which belong to you in the world of reality".[5] The words "for the time being" are important; later, obviously, the insights so gained may profoundly affect one's attitude to the world of reality, and the mystic would go beyond this to claim himself in touch with the Reality of all realities.

Poet and mystic, however, would agree that they move away from the outer forms in which life expresses itself towards some form of transcendent experience. Both are convinced that this inner life is an incomparably rich possession and that no amount of scientific progress or technological advance can take its place in the scope of fully human development.

They are aware that psychologists are rightly concerned to study the processes and phenomena of creativity, and have noted that some investigators are convinced that there are no adequate grounds for supposing that further research will not uncover causal explanations of creativity within their own terms. It may indeed become increasingly possible to distinguish measurable aspects of the creative process, classifying and systematizing them within the world of empirical reality. But there is surely room for the viewpoint that creativity—and the contemplative attitude which fosters it—remains vaster and deeper than any explanation the measuring processes may attempt to give.

Analytical methods of the kind usually available to psychologists must necessarily be concerned with formulation of that which *is*, but it is a key feature of creativity in any form that it is always open-ended. "Reality approached from art", says Etienne Gilson, "is being in the sense in which becoming is being", for the artist is "in quest of forms which only his own free choice can determine".[6]

In fact the artist in any field epitomizes the tension between order and freedom which is a commonplace in Christian theology. He must continually throw off the apparently orderly framework of observed external reality and socializing process and commit himself to "an infinite awareness of the continuously changing panorama of inner and outer events".[7] He will exchange established security for a much profounder sense of order, dimly perceived and often painfully unattainable within the current limitations of his vision. But it is a bargain he gladly makes. Timothy Leary, one-time Professor of Psychology at Harvard, now convicted under the

American drug laws, explains the readiness—"no longer need he impose on the inner world of his receptive awareness the terms he uses to describe external events. He can go out beyond categorizing modes to the recovery of direct perceptual experience, beyond complete commitment to the world he touches and feels to an infinitely expanded universe", beyond the language of intellectual speculation and practical demonstration to "the oldest language in the world—the non-verbal language of spontaneous dance, painting, sculpture; the verbal language of religion, poetry, song, myth, esoterics; the abstract language of mysticism".[8]

Here, in this definition, artist and mystic find themselves side by side. But it would be wrong to argue from this either that aesthetic experience is a substitute for religious experience, or that creative art must be valued mainly as a stepping-stone to spiritual apprehension. Aesthetic experience, either creative or responsive, is wholly valid and valuable in its own right. We do scant justice to poetry, for example, if we regard it either as a substitute for religion or its handmaid. But aesthetic experience has analogies with religious experience; the aesthetic attitude and the contemplative can be mutually sympathetic and interpretative. If we value the aesthetic experience, we find that it adds to life a rich dimension which is not patient of purely scientific explanation. We may then be less inclined to dismiss the experience and teaching of the spiritual masters, and less disturbed when their insights also fail the tests of verification which some scientists and even some few theologians would impose.

CREATIVE INSPIRATION AND PROCESS

The actual *processes* of aesthetic creation show a similarly significant correspondence with the lines along which spiritual insight may develop.

There is fortunately an increasing body of material in which the inner workings of inspiration may be studied. Psychologists have begun to concern themselves most fruitfully with the study of creativity; the reports, for instance, of successive Conferences of Creativity Research at Utah offer papers on most diverse subjects, ranging from selective testing for work requiring a high degree of originality to controlled experiments in drug-taking as a source of artistic creation.

Sixteen years ago, Brewster Ghiselin edited *The Creative Process*, subtitled a "revealing study of genius at work". This fascinating collection of excerpts from autobiographical accounts of the making of poetry, paintings, musical compositions, and so on has stimulated production of other anthologies in the same field. Writers by trade have always tended to turn their sensitive awareness in upon themselves, and there is of course a rich mine of autobiographical material of varying shapes and sizes; but the increasingly self-conscious interest in creative process has led musicians and artists also to explore the internal and external stresses which help or hinder the production of original work.

The inner world of religious experience has been well documented for centuries. The subject easily provokes a certain exhibitionism of the Madame Guyon type, but the necessity of seeking and giving guidance at all levels of Christian life has left us with valid and authentic material which is often amazingly precise and perceptive.

Thus the new and surely rewarding factor is the opportunity we now have of comparing a great variety of accounts of the inner life, whether its particular context be artistic or religious.

The details, both of carefully observed case-histories and of highly personalized self-revelatory writings, vary enormously. But certain general principles of creative inspiration and activity seem to be discernible.

Basic to the whole process is the creative urge. The true artist is driven by an internal necessity. Kandinsky distinguishes three strands in this. There is the element of personality, arising from the artist's necessity to express himself; the element of style, by which the artist is impelled to express the spirit of the age; and the element of "quintessential art", fruit of the desire to express the eternal and objective in terms of the historical and subjective. Of these strands, he regards the last as the most important, imposing on the artist the necessity of ignoring the demands of mere popularity or contemporaneity in order that he may "watch his own inner life and hearken to the demands of internal necessity",[9] a necessity which clearly requires a great purity of artistic intention.

One can multiply quotations on the same theme. "The obligation of art is a categorical imperative uttered to ourselves by ourselves", writes C. J. Ducasse, "the obligation imposed by the law of one's own being".[10] Stephen Spender speaks of "a spiritual compulsion",[11] Thomas Wolfe of a book which "took hold of me and possessed me".[12] It is significant that four-and-a-half years elapsed before the book which took hold of Thomas Wolfe appeared on the publisher's desk.

The motivation of any creative artist must be not only strong, but sustained. "Inspiration is not only the impulse which sets creation in motion; it is also the energy which keeps it going—the energy to bear on every detail of the work as well as, constantly, on the whole".[13]

The Christian who seriously prays is conscious of the same imperatives, of a grace which comes "not merely as an impulse to the soul, but as a light and fire that can grow indefinitely in power and take possession of all the faculties of man".[14] The more profound his understanding of vocation, the more he recognizes that God is always the seeker, the initiator, and also that it is only by the progressive and patient reorientation of his whole life that he will in fact achieve his true individual purpose. He also needs great purity of intention; and perhaps a particular watchfulness at the present time lest he over-value the importance of contemporaneity in his religious approach.

Though the initial urge must thus be maintained by discipline at every successive stage of the creative activity, nothing can on occasion look less disciplined than the raw material which goes into the finished work.

The great artist has a stored mind and a stored imagination. He is never too old or too proud to learn. He often takes conscious steps to feed his imagination on specified subjects. Julian Levi, painter of seascapes, extended his knowledge of the sea by every means available to him, even to the point of learning to sail. "The musical mind", says Harold Shapiro, "cannot begin to function in a creative way until it has absorbed a considerable variety of tonal experiences".[15] The poet or novelist studies many different styles before he evolves his own.

To refuse to learn, to soak oneself in background knowledge and impressions, dries up the sources upon which inspiration can subconsciously work. It is perhaps not wholly irrelevant to remark that many contemporary Christians are apt to be ill-grounded in the traditions and doctrines of their faith, and ill-disposed to learn them. If merely the tag-ends of childish devotion, the recipes of radio religion, and an over-simplified and eclectic collection of biblical stories are fed into the mind's storage system, it is no wonder that the resulting conscious religious attitude is disconcertingly thin in texture and peripheral to the personality. In more religiously sophisticated circles, undue attachment to controversial reading matter can induce a similarly shallow outlook.

The visions and locutions experienced by saints of a less self-conscious age than our own and the flashes of compelling insight which seem more characteristic of present day illumination have often had most powerful results; but they do not appear out of nothing. Under grace, they highlight and creatively synthesize features of a landscape already well-known and explored in depth.

The creative artist also lays himself open to a conscious enhancement of his already marked sensitivity. The intensity of his sense-impressions will be matched by a depth of imaginative sympathy and awareness. The painful process of allowing all one's faculties and perceptions to remain alert and sharp is an inescapable part both of authentic creativity and of spiritual growth.

There have been some doubtful experiments in the systematic expansion of consciousness, undertaken and observed under clinical conditions. Some have led to a considerable degree of heightened aesthetic sensibility and appreciation, though the carry-over from the drugged state to full consciousness is in most cases only limited. An increased sense, for instance, of the visual beauty of the world has been noted as an effect of the drug psilocybin.[16] Various forms of sensory deprivation have also been used to explore similar effects on the expansion of consciousness.

The genuine value of such methods to the artist can be called in question, quite apart from the often deadly danger involved. All such people exhibit an unusual sensitivity, and the processes of artificial enhancement will not make a creative giant out of an averagely competent, responsible, and unimaginative man-in-the-street. No more will the physical disciplines of fasting and vigil make a saint out of anyone who employs them. Women who fast to save their waistlines are not necessarily saving their souls thereby.

But the wealth—and sometimes the terror—of the imagery evoked by drug-taking and the increased sensitivity which may follow prolonged fasting does at least suggest than many of us may be capable of a greater richness of imaginative and perceptual experience than, in the interests of physical health, mental security, or spiritual safety, we allow ourselves to accept.

There is, of course, wisdom in this, and we are often subconsciously aware of the limits of our tolerance; but do we perhaps set our threshold of endurance too low? "Eight hours sleep and three square meals a day are adequate safeguards of comfortable living, but it may be questioned whether the Kingdom of Heaven suffers any violence by such a regime!"[17]

In any case, artificially produced enhancements of consciousness are obviously not the same thing as the delicate and subtle impressionability of a man who is sufficiently disciplined to handle his awareness. After twenty-one years I still remember vividly that what appeared to be one of the richest and most significant insights I have ever had accompanied the birth under anaesthetic of our second child, but the carry-over into volitional life was almost negligible.

Nevertheless, certain so-called "civilizing" and adaptive pressures hinder sanctity as well as creativity, and both saints and artists easily attract the gibe of madman. Some indeed, artistically gifted beyond the capacity for endurance, slip over the border. A modern painter, speaking of Van Gogh, precisely states the problem: "to the psychologist it is the periodic insanity of Van Gogh that is pre-eminent, and the psychologist induces much from that. But to the artist it is clear that *it was the great love of things and people* and the incredible *suffering* which made his art possible and his insanity inevitable".[18] A modern writer on mysticism underlines the same point—"the soul destined for great things may be psychologically infirm. It may even be possible, though it cannot be asserted, that the delicacy of the natural organism needed for the reception of spiritual energy is such that it has weaknesses that can be repaired only by spiritual force".[19]

The great Christian as well as the great artist knows and experiences the creativity of suffering and the relationship of love and pain. It is part of the central pattern of his conviction, to be evaded only at the expense of his vocation.

Between the initial creative urge, acting on a mind rich both in knowledge and awareness, and the finished product there seems to lie a state of confusion and "indeterminate fullness",[20] a "whirling vortex and creative chaos".[21] Varying periods of gestation are required before this kaleidoscope of impressions, images, memories, and emotions can be pressed into service. The pause which necessarily precedes creation allows the material to be absorbed and assimilated, though with little attempt at conscious synthesis or categorizing. The material is, as it were, held in solution, in a state of "imaginative muddled suspense",[22] waiting for months or maybe for years until the form of the new work or new insight is revealed.

Artists behave differently during this process of absorption and assimilation. For some, the absorption is more or less unconscious and the beginning of the creative work is touched off by some quite often extraneous stimulus. Others work intermittently with ideas thrust up out of the chaos, going as far as inspiration allows and resuming after a further period of gestation. Most will refine, polish, and correct the work done in a type of "final verification" process.

The one fact which clearly emerges from their several experience is that they cannot, as it were, force their inspiration into any channel of clear, logical development. They cannot produce the required result by any of the usual processes of ordered thought and mental clarification. They must in fact learn to accept with patience a condition of non-attachment, non-involvement. They must move away from concern with particular detail and preoccupation with particular aspects of their accumulated material.

Etienne Gilson summarizes this condition as "the long and ascetic preparation that precedes artistic creation", having for its object "the elimination of obstacles—perceptions, images, imitational urges, acquired habits, even skills—standing in the way of new germinal form and its materialization".[23]

It is not, however, a state of slackness, open to any and every invasion from the subconscious level; it is a state of "extreme watchfulness, collectedness, unfocussed consciousness".[24] Even moments of insight bearing on the ultimate production must be held "without insistence, without attachment", but with a profound quality of awareness. Evelyn Underhill, commenting on a similar state as it affects contemplatives, emphasizes that for them also this still watchfulness is never sloth : "No temperament is less slothful than the mystical one, and the 'quiet' to which the mystics must school themselves in the earlier stages of contemplation is often the hardest of their tasks. The abandonment of lucid intellectual activity is only undertaken in order that they may, as Plotinus describes it, 'energize enthusiastically upon another plane' ".[25] In speaking of that benighting of the intellect characteristic of the passive night of the senses, St John of the Cross warns that a man in this state "should not desire to apply his judgement in order to know the nature of his own condition or feelings, or the nature of such and such a vision, motion, or feeling".[26]

Later, some may move into a general and more or less continuous state of recollection, a loving awareness of God underlying every aspect of their daily life, a source of knowledge and insight, of wisdom and an overflowing charity. But any conscious effort to acquire this, even for the most apparently reputable reasons, would be self-defeating. The love of God floods in as self-concern, introspection, and interior chatter are dropped, because there are then no obstacles to its action. A soul dispossessed of itself is ready to be possessed by God; with a naked intent stretching towards God, it loves God with his own love in so far as love of self is starved and eliminated.

John Ruysbroeck in one breath-taking sweep of description indicates the qualities of the God-seeing man, linking Christian action and contemplation in decisive phrases. "His outer life of sense must be well disposed and ordered in good works before the eyes of all men. His inner life must be full of grace and charity, unfeigned, with right intention and rich in all virtues. His memory, freed from care and solicitude, should be free and empty, *delivered from all images*. His heart should be free, open, and raised above all the heavens; his intellect free from reflections and naked in God. This is the citadel of loving spirits, where all pure intelligences are re-united in a simple purity".[27]

The self finds itself in a curiously paradoxical state. On the one hand there is an attempt to shed every scrap of role-playing, anything which would dull perception, as in Stephen Spender's insistence that one must "achieve nakedness, be all that one is . . ."; on the other hand, there must be an open-eyed surrender of self, a "casting loose of the ties of security", a self-surrender calling for a "purity of motive that is rarely sustained save through dedication and discipline".[28]

It is hardly surprising that this state, so easily recognized and authentically described both by creative artist and contemplative, should exhibit the note of paradox. Psychologists studying creativity are aware that the creation of something new, the unusual flash of integration is a "genuine resolution or synthesis of certain common antinomies" and that "the basis of all antinomies is that arising from the distinction between the self and the not-self".[29] To be both self-aware and self-surrendered, completely fulfilled and yet freed from the dominance of the ego, is the paradoxical end-term of selfhood which can be grasped by experience, but not demonstrated by argument. It is an experience shared by genius and saint, and recognized in less developed form by artists and contemplatives who know themselves to be neither.

THE END PRODUCT

The rewards for this surrender, this leap in the dark, vary according to the sustained seriousness of purpose which underlies the commitment. At one end of the scale we have the transitory effect of certain types of drugs, described as "the loss of ego without vulnerability", the sense of enjoying "a pure state of being".[30] At the other end, speaking from a Christian standpoint, is the state of being "stripped, transformed, transparent, enflamed with love in the darkness, filled with a supernaturally simple light, pure, general, detached from every particular",[31] ready, in fact, in the words of St Paul, to be a partaker of the inheritance of the saints in light. Between lie all the experiments with drugs for scientific investigation, for the healing of ills both physical and mental, the planned expansion of consciousness for the purposes of artistic creation.

There will obviously be differences of opinion on the use and misuse of drugs as a means of enlightenment; a difference high-lighted by recent criminal proceedings in the United States. The Christian cannot readily avoid the conclusion that, for the creative artist as well as for himself, a surrender made by the whole personality, fully conscious and wholly willed,

has the merit of being not only free from the obvious psychological risks, but inherently the most fruitful. There is a
proper distinction to be made between a trance-like state
which may result from courageous creative discipline,
whether in an artistic or a religious context, and the trance
deliberately induced for the purpose of creative work or
illumination.

In both spheres, the aspect of the surrender which calls
forth all available resources of courage and commitment is
the darkness which surrounds it and the obscurity of the end
result. A man must surrender open-eyed to a process of
creation or growth whose end he does not see and whose
workings he may not fully understand at the time.

This is not to suggest that the leap in the dark is unselective.
The creative process is highly selective, but it will be fluid
and sensitive to deviations from the *rightness* which the artist
envisaged in his first conception. "The picture", says Picasso,
"is not thought out and determined beforehand; rather while
it is being made it follows the mobility of thought".[32] A painting is both creative and responsive, "an intimately communi-
cative affair between painter and painting, between idea
and image".[33] The composer bears witness to the same elusive
balance between conscious control and instinctive sensibility
to the developing form itself—"working at his music, he is
not so much conscious of his ideas as possessed by them.
Very often he is unaware of his exact processes of thought
till he is through with them; extremely often the completed
work is incomprehensible to him immediately after it is
finished: his experience in creating the work is incalculably
more intense than any later experience he can have from
it".[34] The artist in fact has a sense of direction in general, but
often no consciousness of the route.

Similarly, the contemplative's quest for truth takes him into
the cloud of unknowing; "in order to arrive at that which
thou knowest not, thou must go by a way that thou knowest
not".[35] He comes face to face with the light of infused knowledge which is a ray of darkness to him.

For the artist, the reward of this kind of creative discipline, persevered with and endured, is the production of work with a degree of beauty, order, and universality which uses his personal experience to reach conclusions of much wider validity. The subjective and objective are fused, the intense personal experience is transmuted by creative genius into something of universal significance. The chaotic material assembled in the early stages of creative inspiration becomes an inherently orderly statement, has an authenticity beyond any mechanically computerized or statistically gathered material, a recognizable simplicity and clarity, a wholeness which critics may analyse, but which is far more than the particular details and forms into which they may break it up.

According to the degree of his own awareness and sensitivity, the man who listens to music, reads or hears poetry, looks at paintings or other forms of plastic creation, is admitted to the experience of the artist himself. He never reaches the point of sharing the creative stress, but often achieves a relative degree of self-forgetting absorption and attention, which bears some resemblance to the processes of the original inspiration.

Thus the work, conceived and executed by a particular man at a particular period becomes a possession for all men at all times.

But at the summit of the mystic's ladder, the man chosen and laid hold of by God in eternal, personal love finds not only universal significance, but the Universal Source. He is enfolded by the mutual life-giving contentment of the Trinity. "Upon this contentment", says Ruysbroeck, "depend heaven and earth, and life and being, and the activity and preservation of all creatures—and from it grace and glory and all gifts pour forth in heaven and on earth, and into each creature separately, according to its needs and receptivity". The saint is in fact introduced into the Trinitarian source of universal life, where "all things are consummated, all things are wrought", and wherein lie "the power and possibilities of all things".[36]

Is this stupendous vision different in quality from the artist's, or merely an exalted development of artistic awareness, feeding on religious rather than aesthetic concepts?

It is perhaps in answer to this question that the testimony of one particular creative artist bears more extended comment, offering a useful introduction to those factors which, in the final resort, differentiate artistic and spiritual disciplines.

It is Henry Miller, in his *Reflections on Writing*, who uses the term "leap in the dark" to describe the act of self-surrender essential to the creative process. "I had to grow foul with knowledge, realize the futility of everything, grow desperate, then humble, then sponge myself off the slate as it were, in order to recover my authenticity. I had to arrive at the brink and then take a leap in the dark".[37] St Catharine of Siena uses similar words to express the moment of truth when the soul ceases to measure itself against others of its kind but against a glimpse of the Reality of God. She hears God speak of the valley of humility in which "thou wilt know Me and thyself—in self-knowledge then thou wilt humble thyself, seeing that, in thyself, thou dost not even exist".[38]

Face to face with his own vision of reality, Henry Miller knows that it is "something he grasps rather than learns; as he learns less, he realizes more"; he learns in "some different, more subterranean way"; he acquires "the gift of immediacy". He develops "the ability to perceive, apprehend, analyse, synthesize, categorize, inform, stimulate—all at once".[39]

This gift of immediacy, of simultaneous apprehension, is typical also of illumination in the spiritual field, the state of heightened consciousness which so often is the fruit of contemplative discipline—at first an intoxicating joy, only much later and after many vicissitudes steadying down into the knowledge of the Trinity in Unity as the fruit and end of all our life. "The things which the seer brings back with him when he returns to common life are not merely partial impressions, or the separate knowledge of 'science' or 'poetry'.

They are truths which embrace the world—in a word, the whole consciousness".[40]

The greater the certitude the less the ability to communicate and describe it in any direct terms. "Simplicity", says Miller, "is the fruit of perception", and yet "with increasing simplification the mystery heightens and what I know tends to become more and more unstateable". Simplicity and significance go hand in hand at the highest levels of artistic inspiration, and yet neither words, nor colour and form, nor musical sound suffice to plumb the depths of the simplicity nor expose the vastness of the significance. Even so the contemplative enters into the "cloud of unknowing", for the movement from appearances into reality is a movement away from the clear-cut and the communicable into darkness for the intellect and a contact with the infinite which beggars all known modes of description and suggestion.

Miller describes the effect of his own experience upon his personality. He lives in certitude, "not dependent on proofs or faith". Like the mystic, he "knows". Unlike the mystic, he lives completely for himself, "without the least egotism or selfishness", because he is "abetting the scheme of things". He drops below the surface of a life where all is conceived in terms of money and power, sinks and disappears from sight into a state *where life really begins*. He achieves a "condition of sublime indifference", which he himself terms a logical development of the egocentric life. And yet, having "lived out the social problem by dying, he can write or not write, devoid of any sense of compulsion, dropping his fruits like a ripe tree, doing all out of sheer joy". He makes his life "in accord with the deep-centred rhythm of the cosmos". "Paradise", he concludes, "is everywhere; and every road, if one continues along it far enough, leads to it".

Is the essential quality of his experience so very different from the "condition of complete simplicity, costing not less than everything" of which T. S. Eliot spoke? Is his grasp of the fact that mystery is not to be pierced by understanding but absorbed by acceptance, "living with it, in it, through it, and by it", so very far apart from the much-quoted remark of the author of *The Cloud of Unknowing*: "By love may he be gotten and holden, but by thought never"? "Even art", says Miller, being really accepted, "will cease to be, for it is only a symbol language for something which can be seized directly". "For we know in part", answers St Paul, "and we prophesy in part, but when that which is perfect is come, then that which is in part shall be done away".

The correspondences, the analogies, are startling—evidence enough that the sum of human experience is far greater and more profound than that which is patient of purely scientific investigation. But we may not push the analogies further than they can profitably go.

It would be quite wrong to flourish Henry Miller's moving self-revelation as describing an approximation to Christian contemplative experience which unaccountably got no further. His experience is in no sense secondrate; it stands in its own right as the essential condition of valid creative work: as such, what he and other artists have to say underlines the splendid vitality and flexibility of the imaginative life, both its freedom and its innate resistance to any kind of scientific formulation.

But, for the Christian, of necessity the chief end of artistic creation differs from the chief end of man. Artistic experience is concerned with the relationships of the created world. It attempts to express these relationships and terminates in a work of self-expression, however great and universal its significance. Spiritual experience is concerned with the relationships between the created world and the Creator, and terminates not in any kind of utterance, but in silence, the silence of worship which is the ultimate response to an utterance, a Word, not human but divine.

The creative urge is not the same thing as the passion for the Absolute which dominates the consciousness of the true contemplative. Both defy scientific analysis and demand an unrelenting discipline: both impose pain, yet promise an astounding fruition and joy.

But even the most exalted literary form, even the most "contemplative" of music, whether it be the Arietta of Beethoven's piano sonata, Opus III, or Barraque's contemporary exploration of the role of silence in music, remains within the realm of nature. It is inspired utterance, revealing with unusual plenitude and transparency the relationships and the being of the natural world. Because we are ourselves part of the natural world, we can be powerfully worked upon by any communication which seems to render luminous the nature and experience of the world of which we form a part. Therefore, though aesthetic creation can never be a substitute for religion, it can at certain stages have a marked effect upon religious experience radiated through natural means.

But the direct encounter of God and man to which all religion aspires takes place in the order of grace, in the world of the supernatural. The vision of God is inaccessible to nature unassisted by grace; not even the most sublime composition can bring us face to face with God, but even a very little love can set us on our way thither.

It is important to notice, as a recent critical study points out, that Miller's state of "abiding peace, the peace of God and serene security created by a handful of good neighbours living at one with the creature world",[41] is in effect a community of "lone travellers", men who are good neighbours because along paths of anarchy and rebellion they have acquired the supreme confidence of men who know where they stand.[42]

Strangely, it is the modern novelist who here retreats from the world, seeing his Utopia in the almost primitively simple community at Big Sur, which turns its back upon the mechanistic, scientifically oriented world in which most of us must move.

How profoundly one sympathizes with his criticism of the modern world in which "our thoughts, our energies, our very lives are being used up to create what is unwise, unnecessary, unhealthy".[43] And yet Miller had to experience this life compulsively as a violent, uninhibited whole, then to escape from it, and then to discover himself in fact inhibited by his own non-acceptance of the pitiful, inhibited world. At bottom, his ideal community was artificial and illusory, and he knew it— just as he knew that even there neither he nor his follow "loners" could escape the weight of their own problems, whether of personal relationships or of personal realization.

He moves out of his retreat and no longer rages against the world "because to rage is to be non-accepting". With some perplexity he speculates that the most effective way of communicating with the world may be the way of stored wisdom, of sanctity—a communication by being.

It is these men, reflects Miller, the wise and the holy, who know that "we have our being in utter mystery"; and it is they, mute, withdrawn, often unknown . . . who affect us immeasurably".[44]

Why?

The saint himself, for all his natural tendency to silence and obscurity, is sometimes forced into articulateness, against his will, in spite of himself. He then gives us, because he has lived it, the answer we can only take on trust.

Silouan, Staretz of Athos, wrote no books and stayed in his appointed place, but others sought him there and pressed him to speak. From his own notes and from conversations with him, his disciple, Sofrony, built up a picture of this God-seeing man.

He is the one to whom being and loving are synonymous, but, because he loves with Christ's love, he experiences both "a blessedness with which nothing in this world can compare" and at the same time "a suffering greater than any other suffering". He communicates by being because, in experiencing the mystery of Christlikeness, he "reaches the core of his own being and looking into it sees that the existence of mankind is not something alien and extraneous to him, but is inextricably bound up with his own existence".[45]

"Our brother is our life", says Silouan,[46] and he thus accepts *in himself* all his brother's sin and suffering, becoming, through his own intense responsiveness to Christ, a redemptive force.

The final state in the long process of Christian detachment and sanctification is thus that of the *alter Christus*, dying in the world, through the world and for the world, not necessarily the death of the martyrs, but the daily dying of which St Paul speaks.

This is as true of contemplative withdrawal as of active charitable work, as I have tried to show. Any Christian, whatever his state of life, must, as Bouyer has finely said, "hate the world as it is because we must love the world as God wills it".[47] But this process does not isolate him; it brings him into the forefront of the battle, even though at certain stages for all men and for much of their lives for some men the battle is fought secretly and in solitude. "Thy kingdom come" is part of the earliest prayer we learn: they plumb its depths who seek the King, and thus, whether in obvious involvement or in frequently misunderstood detachment, set forth the salvation of all men.

The world, for all its horror, its suffering, its trifling with atomic disaster, is firmly anchored in the will of God and in his redemptive purpose. To be one with God is thus not only to be one with oneself but to be one with the world; the way to true identity is through a self-loss so profound that no external circumstance or fear can hinder the continual exercise of love.

It is the goal of the artist to experience and illumine the inner correspondences of life, using techniques and accepting disciplines which the contemplative recognizes and understands. In a technologically oriented age, the authenticity of the aesthetic attitude is a continual bastion against the shrinkage of human capacity. But the contemplative points an even profounder moral. Let the poet who is also the contemplative have the final word:

But to apprehend
The point of intersection of the timeless
With time, is an occupation for the saint—
No occupation either, but something given
And taken, in a lifetime's death in love.

T. S. ELIOT, *The Dry Salvages.*

9

Authentic Worship

THE MYSTERY

We now perhaps reach the crucial question. We may accept the view that the contemplative attitude needs to be taken more seriously in the field of modern theological debate. We may even note with relief that poets and artists find the language of contemplation wholly respectable and meaningful. But has it any relevance for the ordinary workaday Christian, the average worshipper, who goes to Church fairly regularly, makes his communion rather more often now his local vicar has made it the main Sunday service, and tries to do the decent thing in the week? I would answer most emphatically, "Yes, and especially *now*!"

There is one significant difference between artistic and religious genius. Vocation and commitment are common both to aesthetic and religious discipline, but the artist often stops short at one vital point. He is not essentially required to assume an attitude of worship. The Christian, whether beginner or saint, must.

Therefore, the average worshipper, by the very fact of his worship, is grasping the basic truth of his life as a Christian. It is therefore to him above all that contemplation is relevant. A grasp of what the contemplative attitude really means can link his personal spiritual life and his Sunday worship, can deliver him from the "Church over against the world" dichotomy, and can turn his somewhat defensive "I'm no saint" attitude into the conviction that in the long run sanctity is the only worth-while object of his life, and the most perfect service he can offer to his fellows. For worship means more than appreciation, understanding, even reverence. It means the acceptance of creatureliness in the presence of the Creator, and that is what the contemplative attitude is about. It envisages therefore a total response to a total demand.

Further, in the Christian Church, it not only invites but also demands that this response shall be made in the context of the Eucharist, the supreme act of worship in time and the supremely guaranteed link with eternity. The contemplative attitude therefore finds both its source and its fulfilment in the sacramental life of the Church.

There are unfortunately two current attitudes which seem to drive a wedge between contemplative experience and the worshipping life of the Church.

In the first place, there is a tendency to isolate the contemplative, still more the mystic, from the life of the Church as a whole. He is regarded as a peripheral type, an eccentric, someone specially gifted—or handicapped. He is frequently misrepresented as a "loner" who draws little from and contributes still less to the day-to-day life of the Christian community.

In the second place, the relationship between worship and works is obscured in a pragmatic age which is passionately activist and tends, even in ecclesiastical circles, to judge by results.

We thus find ourselves with a growing tension between the ideas of worship and service, a tension which colours every aspect of the Church's work, and possibly comes to a head in the pastoral situation on the issue of the conduct of eucharistic worship .

Behind much current liturgical controversy there seems to lie a fundamental unease and uncertainty as to the balance to be struck between prayer and life, worship and work. Mutual distrust and incomprehension feed on this basic insecurity of outlook.

The individual member of the Church easily loses his sense of direction. Some, nurtured in a more settled tradition, retire into an inner life which but grudgingly accepts any changes in worship or Church life in general. They struggle on or give up, as the case may be, but they feel out-moded and out of touch, clinging to a hardly-won pattern and yet finding their own devotional life going sour. Others are led on by the cry for involvement to give more than their inner resources will stand, until they too find themselves frustrated and frightened.

The one group fears and distrusts the secularization of Christianity; the other makes much of the ivory tower image. One is accused of worshipping a God "out there"; the other is suspected of disposing of him altogether. A true grasp of the context of the contemplative attitude is surely crucial to this currently strained situation.

Even at the lowest level of our understanding of the nature of the Church, we must see it as a body of many members, bringing, by their incorporation into Christ, their several gifts to the service of the whole. In an age beleaguered by the forces of secularism (and worse) the Church cannot afford a division of purpose. Each must give according to capacity, recognizing the partial and limited nature of his giving and its need to be supplemented by the complementary talents of others.

But there is a much deeper level of apprehension of the doctrine of the Body of Christ which shows that not only must contemplative and "doer" respect each other, but that they are incomplete on their own, since specifically Christian life is that of contemplation issuing in action, because it is centred on the Eucharist, the saving action of God in Christ.

At the heart of the Church's life, therefore, we are presented neither with a code of ethical conduct nor with a programme of social reform, however exalted; we are offered a mystery. This is the mystery of God's saving purpose enacted in and through the Cross of our Lord, and re-enacted in, by, and for the Church in the Eucharist.

This mystery—*the* Mystery of the Christian faith—is wholly given and revealed as God's economy of salvation, and wholly objective and realistic, being in no way dependent on our grasp of it.

In fact it is only participation in the Mystery which will enhance our subjective capacity to grasp it. The appropriate attitude is contemplative, the appropriate reaction is surrender, the appropriate response is praise. Contemplation and worship are inseparable aspects of our attendance at the Eucharist. As we worship, we are drawn closer to that which we contemplate. We are in fact incorporated into the saving action of God in Christ, and we accept our destiny to become through love and sacrifice the instruments whereby the Mystical Body of Christ is made whole.

There would seem to be two corollaries of this assertion.

In the first place, the Eucharist is not primarily a service of "mission". It is the central act of worship of the believing Church, a mystery whose significance becomes the more apparent as it is entered into with greater faith and surrender. It should inspire and nourish missionary activity, but it cannot by its nature be immediately and wholly accessible to all comers.

The man who is beginning to discover the world of music will go to concerts and listen to records, knowing that he will thus be progressively initiated into realms of delight and appreciation hitherto hidden from him: but he will not expect to understand and fully penetrate the structure and significance of any musical composition the first time he hears it. He is led forward partly by his own growing conviction that here is an aspect of life which has much to offer, and partly by the testimony of others who persuade him that he may ultimately derive an exultant and richly creative sense of discovery from works which initially make little appeal. In any field it is a shallow range of experience which holds no rewards for deeper exploration and commitment.

In the second place, Eucharistic worship is not peripheral, an optional extra for the devout. As the increasing tendency to set the Eucharist at the centre of the Church's worshipping life demonstrates, it is at the very heart of our personal commitment. Moreover I believe it dictates the terms of that commitment in a way which makes it abundantly clear that there is no tension between the inner life and the liturgical life of the Christian, no conflict between comtemplative experience and sacramental grace.

As Christians we say with St Paul that it is our vocation to make up what is lacking in the sufferings of Christ. And this is no melodramatic exaggeration; it is a sober statement of fact. The Church is the instrument of God's purpose of redemption, living with his life and extending his kingdom to all mankind. It is for this purpose that each individual worshipper is baptized into the Body of Christ and fed with his Body and Blood.

But how can he hope to be made fit to accomplish in some small and limited way his part in this work? He cannot do it merely by attending church services, he cannot do it by making his communion as a routine observance. He cannot even do it by immersing himself in the service of his neighbour, since even the service of others, pursued in our own way, can issue in and from remarkably egocentric attitudes. He can only do it by such a spiritually prepared participation in the Sacrament that Christ may have his way with him and through him with all men. "I live, yet not I but Christ liveth in me".

Life and liturgy must become one single response of love, in which ascetic preparation, sacramental grace, and persevering discipleship bring us into an increasingly profound relationship with God and with all men. Purity of intention will blend with purity of action, and love will have its perfect work.

The struggle for perfection thus becomes an imperative, not because we should like to be saints—which is on the whole a daunting prospect—but because we can do no other than offer to God for his purpose "ourselves, our souls and bodies, to be a reasonable, holy and lively sacrifice". Sanctity is closeness to God, whether experimentally, that is to say mystically, apprehended or not. What is certain is that it will demand an ever increasing degree of detachment and discipline, and that it will flower in ever increasing generosity of service.

Only in this context can the quality of the discipline and the service be safeguarded—by a love which can be progressively freed from emotionalism and self-interest because it reflects in some measure the love of the Cross.

"I lose myself, wondering at him" is the essence of the contemplative vision; it is also the prerequisite of all right action. "It is in fact", says Mascall boldly, "in simply being itself and living its own supernatural life that the Church performs its greatest service to the world"[1]

THE LITURGY

If the Eucharist is the dynamic centre of the Church's life, the characteristic activity of the Body of Christ, it will itself dictate some of the terms of liturgical presentation.

In other words, any liturgical renewal which starts even subconsciously from the manward end is likely to reach wrong conclusions. We start from this end if we are unduly concerned that worship should be directed towards results, whether the aim be evangelism, instruction, social betterment, or even entertainment. One hopes that worship will in fact achieve all these separate aims, either directly or indirectly, but any one of them specifically sought can obscure the main issue. This may well happen if we take too seriously the suggestion that liturgy should not be imposed on people by authority, but should at least in part arise from below.

To regard the Eucharist primarily as evangelistic angles it to the unbeliever instead of the faithful; to streamline it as a means of instruction leads to over-simplification, to stress its entertainment value opens the door to some inappropriate experiments. Even to intend that it should inspire decent standards of behaviour is to become over-conscious of its social function.

To start from the Godward end is to contemplate a God "in light inaccessible hid from our eyes", and therefore to adore God *because he is God*, transcending, despite the graciousness of the Incarnation, all ideas we can possibly have of him.

The sacraments are the gift of God to man, and they share in this mystery of his being and purpose. The content of a sacrament is an act of God: therefore, though psychological and sociological considerations are obviously of importance to the liturgical reformer, his theological understanding and his spiritual depth are even more relevant. It is interesting that Bouyer, a liturgical scholar to whom reformers have paid considerable attention, insists that the application of lines of rediscovery to actual liturgical practice requires "the soul of a contemplative"[2] as well as pastoral experience and deep biblical and theological learning. Beauduin, whose work in this field at the beginning of the century was decisive, was such a man; Dom Casel of Maria-Laach was also both learned and of deep spirituality. In a time of proliferating experiment these qualifications seem even more important.

I remember for instance the young layman who announced before the beginning of a Parish Communion that "there will be a meeting after this service to see what changes we should like in the liturgy". In the event, it became quite obvious that he, and others of the congregation, were not really capable of distinguishing differences in liturgical presentation from very considerable changes in doctrinal emphasis, and certainly had no idea where in their turn these shifts of emphasis would lead.

If we accept this principle that worship is its own justification, an inevitable consequence of the contemplation of God, it is necessarily numinous.

Much is made nowadays of the homeliness, the intimacy, of the Communion service. There is often a determined effort to domesticate the rite in such a way that it will be generally more at home in a dining-room or even kitchen than in a

traditionally furnished and appointed church. But, in suggesting that the "house Communion" is a more realistic and
genuine act of worship than a traditional assembly in church,
is it not perhaps easy to over-emphasize the phenomenon of
God's gracious manifestation and forget that what he mani-
fests is ineffable mystery? A meal is a homely thing, but the
sacred meal has always carried an extremely rich symbolism.
The essence of the rite is that homely things become vehicles
of the holy, not that the holy is contained and limited by the
homely. Moreover, though there may be special occasions and
circumstances when a house celebration is peculiarly applicable, there are equally some very considerable pastoral difficulties in attempting to make it a norm as many parish priests
will know.

In any case, to strive consciously for domesticity, studied
spareness of presentation, almost casualness in liturgical
worhip could be a sign of naturalistic humanism rather than
of primitive simplicity. Awe is not necessarily subservient or
superstitious.

The core of essential mystery in the Eucharist means too
that we cannot "explain" the liturgy and so reveal its essential
nature. We can and must instruct so that the worshipper can
grasp in some measure what is going on, but understanding
will only take him so far. Even the words of the liturgy have
their limitations; it is the thing done which matters, and this
escapes rational explanation not because it is irrational but
because it is supra-rational. Mystery in this context is not
something we have not yet found out or discovered; it is
something which lies beyond the scope of our present perceptive equipment. Theological learning and biblical scholarship help us to explore the significance of the liturgy, but
stop short always of explanation.

The issue is after all more than one of mere comprehension.
We need to bear in mind, as Dr Dunlop has pointed out, the
distinction between the early and later part of the liturgy,
between the Missa Catechumenorum and the Mass of the
Faithful. The Scripture readings and optional sermon of the

earlier part are intended to make their appeal to the understanding, and to give a species of "common intention" within
fairly wide limits to a congregation's approach to the sacrament itself".[3] But the end and aim of the second part of the
service is not understanding but participation, communion
with God. Here the word is not the vehicle of communication
accessible to the intellect, but the divine Word accessible only
to faith. The language we choose to clothe this mysterious
rite must have in it therefore overtones of poetry and music,
an evocative and suggestible power which will, in this
supreme context, cure words "of the tendency to reduce
everything to themselves".[4]

As a matter of current concern, the desire to add more
pedagogic material to the earlier part of the liturgy, as in
the addition of an Old Testament lesson to the Anglican
Series II service, needs to be balanced by great attention to
the "mysterious density of word and action"[5] in the Anaphora
itself. It is all too easy for this to become scamped and un-
spacious. And to clear away at this point inherent rhythmic
structure and verbal dignity can easily clear away at the same
time the essential element of the numinous. It is a perhaps
not unworthy subsidiary reflection that a casual visitor to a
church service—especially a Communion service—is often
far more profoundly affected by a sense of contact with the
numinous than by a service strictly attuned to an overall
comprehensibility.

It is indeed faith illumined by grace which reaches to the
mystery beyond the words, but the right choice of words can
powerfully aid the process. A very recent and forward-
looking book on prayer is not afraid to suggest that "only
the language of poetry is adequate to articulate a man's consciousness at his most alive and aware".[6]

I would think also that conscious contemporaneity is not
necessarily appropriate in Eucharistic worship. Of course
liturgy must show itself flexible to human need and circumstance, but that is a far cry from the over-adaptation to any

one age of mankind or man which makes it the sport of mere fashion.

The undue modernization of a nun's habit will, in these days of mobile hem-lines, leave her looking dowdy rather than up-to-date—and certainly not very dignified—most of the time. Similarly, the presentation of the Eucharist cannot afford to be modified by every prevailing attitude which temporarily affects popular opinion and culture. The family Eucharist is a splendid ideal and means what it says—that it is a service for every age-group, and for those who expect to worship for three score years and ten. Heavy-handed and frequent changes can be very disturbing to the development of sound religious practice and, more important, of deep spiritual apprehension. And we need to remember that the contemporary distrust of habit is itself partly a reflection at popular level of existentialist philosophy.

Christian revelation is indeed a developing revelation and few would deny the possibility of new insights. But a new thesis with its partial truth must be tested against a revelation which has roots in the past as well as a current presentation, and which also embraces the future. It is the Holy Spirit, not the spirit of the age, which searches the deep things of God. "Newness' in Christian experience is associated with the "new creature", new because made free of eternal life; it is not the newness of novelty.

Nor should we give in too readily to current pressures to adapt liturgical practice to the apparent needs of any one age group. Eric James, for instance, complains that "if liturgical forms are merely imposed, we shall almost certainly auto-matically exclude the majority of teenagers from worship".[7] But if the form is to be an adequate expression of the content, we must expect a liturgy to reflect in some degree the authoritative nature of Christian revelation rather than the principles of democratic procedure.

Moreover, it seems doubtful whether even the most ortho-dox of liturgical forms *automatically* exclude the young. The most healthily mixed congregation I know, including everything from babies in arms to the really aged, and withal very representative of the mixed community in the neighbourhood, has a Parish Communion which does not even use the Series II rite and makes no concessions to ephemeral fads and fancies. But it is a service both lively and reverent, which the young clearly enjoy, which gathers in whole families week after week, and which is patently concerned first and foremost with the worship of God.

On the other hand, my own teenage daughter recently found a Series II Parish Communion so lacking either in dignity or sense of conviction that she flatly refused to attend the same church again. I know that these are two entirely random samples and that it was chance that the second church used Series II and the first one of the more conventional variants of Series I; but I believe it is some indication that we can pay too much attention to modernizing techniques as ready-made answers to the problems of the Church's dealings with the young.

Even if it were true that much of our liturgical practice automatically excludes the teenager, surely the teenager would by the same token be excluded from many other *milieux* where the more mature are perfectly at home? It is surely no compliment to the teenager to suggest that he is quite incapable of selective adaptation. The real drop-out admittedly is a special case. The less unfortunate teenager is as capable of learning and appreciating the techniques of a worthy act of worship as he is of handling the complexities of the hi-fi set or the internal combustion engine.

In any case, mental maturity comes later than physical maturity—spiritual maturity later still. It is perhaps therefore not the wisest thing to conclude that, because the middle-aged, or even the elderly, find certain changes in liturgical presentation upsetting, it is because they are rigid and out-of-touch. Is it just possible that in some cases their experience has brought them more into touch with God? Serenity and spiritual poise are hardly and slowly won, and those who have made any sort of progress along these lines can bring some wisdom into the arena of liturgical debate. The attainment of the fortieth, or even the thirtieth, birthday is not necessarily the first slow stain on the radiance of youthful vision.

Eric James, in the article already quoted, feels that "there is little or no evidence that our liturgical commissions have even begun to include psychological questions in their purview". But it is Jung who stresses that it is in middle age, in fact from forty onwards, that a man is for the first time alone with the crucial problem of success or failure as an individual, since it is at this stage that the protective and more artificial screens of social adaptation fall away. Spiritually, this is a crucial age, with many inhibitions to shed. Some may refuse the challenges and either ossify or opt out into a desperate search for identification with the young. But those Christians who accept them and grow through them are reaching their full stature as individuals and as members of the Church. It seemed to me sad indeed that a recent obituary notice of a splendidly vital Roman Catholic woman of widespread charity and immense initiative and originality should end with the words, "her later years were overcast by her inability to adapt herself with sufficient rapidity to the spate of liturgical change and redistributed doctrinal emphasis which followed in the wake of the second Vatican Council".[8] She was fifty-six.

Further, if contemplation of the central mystery of Eucharistic worship underlies our liturgical thinking, shall we be less likely to trade in supernaturalism in favour of adaptation to a secular environment? Faced by the divine economy of salvation, we cannot dare to strain out from our liturgical practice anything which stresses humility, dependence, deprivation and death.

We may want to use more familiar and commonplace language, but language is evocative, and we are not dealing with commonplace situations.

We may decide to stand for much of the liturgy because we are "God's redeemed people", but the price of that redemption should bring us to our knees. As an American divine recently remarked to me, "I cannot get away from the fact that some of the holiest people in the Bible spent much of their time flat on their faces"!

We may assimilate the form of the liturgy as much as possible to secular models, our ideal being the homely house-church celebration. But if we try to attract by assimilation to the world, may we not be in danger of forgetting that the Church is the redeemed community of the Body of Christ, and that it will serve its purpose in the world in becoming more and more its true self by assimilation to God? Its aim is the imitation of Christ, not the promotion of a public image, however tempting the derivative benefits of the latter may seem.

Finally, I quote two significant remarks from a diocesan directive accompanying a letter sent to every parish urging certain changes in liturgical practice:

"Standing for prayers—especially the chief prayer at Communion—and praying with eyes open is very helpful. *It stops people thinking of having their own private telephone to God.*" (The italics are mine.)

"What shall we gain by changing? We have a better service for joining together. We have an easier service to understand. That means it will be easier for us, and for people not so used to praying, to learn to pray together."

There is rightly a strong emphasis here on corporate activity, but perhaps a tendency to confuse corporateness with conscious togetherness. The corporate nature of the Church is not-spatial and depends neither on numerical strength nor on conscious contiguity.

A husband and wife may sit reading for a whole evening and scarcely exchange a word. This can indicate a marriage at least in the shoals if not on the rocks. But it is more likely to happen where there is a basic companionship so sure and stable that each hesitates to interrupt the other's absorption, though either would be immediately responsive to the other's genuine need. The situation represents the delicacy of adjustment which is typical of a profoundly happy marriage.

Similarly, I would think that "being knit together in one communion and fellowship" is not really equivalent to sociability in worship, and does not depend on continual awareness of the people around one. To pray with one's eyes open is as likely to lead to preoccupation with a neighbour's hat as with her soul, or to entangle one's response to God with one's reaction to the celebrant.

We cannot and should not evade the solitariness of the individual's path to God, whether he prays alone or worships in a congregation. This is not a solitude *à deux* but the solitude of individual response to individual vocation *within* the whole Body. The phrase "private telephone line to God" would seem somewhat to misrepresent the situation in which God lays his hand on our own separate lives and choices.

"Birth and death are solitary; thought and growth are solitary; every final reality of a man's life is incommunicable",[9] wrote Charles Morgan.

Thomas Merton sets the same insight in a more specifically theological context—"It is impossible" for many "to attain to the full likeness of Christ unless they can transcend the limitations of the social group by making the sacrifices demanded of them by the Spirit of Christ, sacrifices which may estrange them from certain of their fellows and force on them decisions of a lonely and terrible responsibility".[10]

This sense of estrangement may at times become part and parcel even of our corporate worship. There are occasions when the familiar external setting of an act of public worship recedes as we are gripped by a sense of overpowering reality, revealing to us more of our own selves as well as some deeper insight into God's purposes. *From there* we go on to a more demanding commitment to and awareness of our neighbour. We often need thus to forget him in order to be taught how to serve him with greater humility and discretion. The liturgical pattern which fails to take account of this has an insufficient grasp of the nature of the relationship between man and God. The ultimate aim of the Christian life is union with Christ, and *through him* with all men. It is not tied to the image of a congregation doing the same things in the same way at the same time.

The Body of Christ has many members and St Paul reminds us that the functions of the members show great variety.

In congregational activity too, as in worship, this individual response needs to be safeguarded. It is not always the wisest thing for a parish priest to press his few daily communicants into the usual round of parish activities, suggesting that they are aloof if they don't join in. Nor is it necessarily true that every faithful parish worker would be better for attending weekday Communion services. Gifts and opportunities differ, and a wise pastor does not attempt to impose the same pattern of worship, activity and witness on all.

The whole of the Christian's life, whether worshipping in church or "going out into the world in the power of thy Spirit" is to be both response and exercise of love through union with God. This comes first; and it demands personal holiness, growth in Christ, and sacramental participation in the life of the Church, his mystical Body. It is only as we commit ourselves to this revelation and communication of his Being that we shall find our own place in the Church and in the world. Our own true identity lies in this participation, and, seeking it there, we comprehend the direct relationship between our irreducible and unprotected selves and all other created beings.

Thus all the activity of the Church in the world is geared to her Eucharistic life, and the expression of that life is determined by the personal, hidden, striving holiness of each individual worshipper. "The purpose of the liturgy", says Louis Bouyer, "is in the final analysis to teach us a life of adoration".[11] This fact will both safeguard its form and determine the manner of our approach.

In Conclusion

———◆———

The proper conclusion of the life of grace is sanctity. But of course sanctity is not an end but a beginning. The saint is apt for use as no lesser man can ever be. Because he has abdicated from himself, he is supple, responsive, aware, ready for all things and all men, for life, and—surprisingly in this day and age—for death.

We tend to flinch at the mention of sanctity. The word carries dramatic and perhaps rather febrile overtones. If we use it at all outside the context of stained glass or hagiography, we certainly hardly associate it with a man or woman we might meet over the counter or in a cinema queue. To see the likeness of Christ in a fellow human being would be altogether too disconcerting.

Feeling that way about the disciple, we not unnaturally prefer a profile to a full-face view of the master. We find it easier to argue about God than to meet his gaze. We prefer the discursive or analytical approach to the old French peasant's "I look at him and he looks at me". And yet he grasped the root of the matter. The loving contemplation of God is our primary concern, and it is necessarily a face-to-face encounter. To it all religious practice leads and from it all fruitful secular involvement flows. Doctrinal discourse exists only to illuminate its significance, worship and prayer to inspire and feed it, Christian action to bring all men within its scope.

The process of assimilation to the God we perceive in this encounter will be slow and often painful even if we keep our eyes firmly fixed on him. But it is halted as soon as we look away; and often at the moment we do look away. We are dazzled by the splendours of scientific development, en meshed in the intricacies of intellectual debate, our sensitivity dulled by materialist ambition or overwhelmed by compassionate concern. Moreover, the world around us is indifferent to what we as Christians have to say, and challenges us to prove our sincerity by what we do.

We are sorely tempted to exchange a reasonable faith for faith in reason, and to let our deeds speak louder than our words. In the long run we find ourselves not at all sure that our words, of belief, conviction, or commitment, might not be better left unspoken. It is but a short step to the interpretation of God's purposes in the light of our own, and, if our projects fail, to the equation of our own distress with the death of God.

Perhaps, both as individuals and corporately as members of the Church, we fail in hope because we distrust the concept of mystery. I have been warned more than once that intelligent present-day Christians fight shy of the word and regard it as a synonym for woolly thinking—or even as carrying sub-Christian undertones. But throughout this study of the contemplative approach I have found the word indispensable. God is a mystery, man is a mystery, the process of redemption is a mystery, our whole future destiny is a mystery, its pattern made available only to faith, hope, and love.

The individual's experience of God is not finally susceptible of formulation and explanation. Intellect is a gift of God, and a faith which does not engage and commit our fullest mental capacity will always remain casual and insecure. But the language of faith goes beyond the language of logical proposition and intellectual debate. It makes use of imaginative insight, symbolism, and poetic analogy, presses into use all the evocative resources of music and art, and finally, having explored the whole gamut of human expressive modes, it falls to silence before the divine inexpressible. This is the moment of stillness when the veil may grow very thin. We may dimly perceive that the perfection asked of us lies in a fusion of creative action and responsive conformity which belongs in the realm of paradox. As we turn from the moment of truth to give ourselves whole-heartedly to the discovery and fashioning of our real identity, we shall find ourselves helped and inspired and instructed by all the finest ventures of the human spirit as well as by the Spirit of God who underwrites them all.

Equally we cannot hope to describe the corporate family life of the Church in terms of a human association or organiz-ation. It is the life of the Body of Christ. The mystery of the Church, to which St Paul bears such perceptive witness, is the mystery of reconciliation, God through Christ reconciling all things to himself, and using in that process every individual Christian according to his capacity.

Unfortunately, the Church's current immense concern with administrative matters tends to obscure her real nature and to confuse and bewilder her members. So much of our energy is drained off in deciding what to do and how to do it that we tend to lose sight of what we are about. Even in Eucharistic worship, where corporate action and individual patterns of prayer and sacrifice should reach their highest joint expres-sion, we are apt to be distracted by change, experiment, and modes of approach which can subtly undermine our faith even in the centrality of the sacramental presence. With the best will in the world and despite all our concern with the notion of encounter, we fail to find the God who meets us there. We downgrade mystery to the level of a puzzle and look in all the wrong places for a solution.

I believe it is only the recovery of a true contemplative attitude in the Church which can establish a demanding relationship with God at the very heart of our religious prac-tice. There are theological lessons to be learned, according to our capacity, and there are services to be accepted and rendered; but the main directive for the Christian is "be ye holy, for I am holy".

The resemblance will take many forms and will take very few of us into a contemplative community, for the wood of our own cross is mostly grown in our garden. But we shall never begin to achieve it at all unless we learn to look and love, expressing our love in the determined bending of our wills to an exacting and humble obedience. In an age of devaluation and diminishing returns, we thus become partners in the one enterprise where total loss is the condition of total gain. Contemplating, we worship; worshipping we offer ourselves; in giving ourselves away we are delivered from the confines of self-possession into the glorious liberty of the children of God.

Notes

NOTES TO PREFACE
1. *The Times*, 25 September 1968
2. *The Times*, 1 September 1970
3. John Robinson, *Honest to God*. S.C.M., 1963, p. 7
4. *Twentieth Century Music—a Symposium*, ed. R. Myers. J. Calder, 1960. Chapter 5, "The Composer and his Audience".

NOTES TO CHAPTER 2
1. *Theological Colleges for Tomorrow*. Church Information Office, & Todd, 1965, p. 65
2. *Church Times*, 1 March 1968

NOTES TO CHAPTER 3
1. Eric Mascall, *The Secularisation of Christianity*. Darton, Longman & Todd, 1965, p. 65
2. Ibid. p. 9
3. Ibid. p. 191
4. Ed. Michael Ramsey, *Christian Spirituality Today*. Faith Press, 1961, p. 5
5. *Spirituality for Today*, ed. Eric James. S.C.M., 1968, p. 95

NOTES TO CHAPTER 4
1 John Robinson, op cit. p. 55
2. Op. cit. p. 100
3. Louis Bouyer, *Introduction to Spirituality*. Desdee Company, 1961, p. 5
4. David Knowles, *What is Mysticism?* Burns and Oates, 1967, p. 26
5. *Spirituality for Today*, p. 172
6. *Church Times*, 17 May 1968
7. *The Times*, May 1968
8. Paul Tillich, Memorial Address for Buber, pub. in *A Reader in Contemporary Theology*, ed. J. Bowden and J. Richmond. S.C.M., 1967, p. 56

9. *Honest to God*, p. 100
10. *What is Mysticism?* p. 133
11. E. W. Trueman Dicken, *The Crucible of Love*. Darton, Longman & Todd, 1963, chapter 2
12. *Acts*, 17.25
13. Ruysbroeck, *The Sparkling Stone*, ed. with *Adornment of Spiritual Marriage* etc. by Evelyn Underhill. John M. Watkins, 1951, pp. 204, 220–1

NOTES TO CHAPTER 5

1. *Spirituality for Tody*, pp. 103–17
2. John Robinson, *The New Reformation?* S.C.M., 1965, p. 98
3. *Christian Spirituality Today*, p. 62
4. John Bernard, O.D.C., in *Mount Carmel*, Vol. 15, No. 4, p. 181
5. *Complete Works of St John of the Cross*, tr. E. Allison Peers. Burns and Oates, 1947, Vol. III, p. 247

NOTES TO CHAPTER 6

1. *Honest to God*, p. 99
2. Margaret Cropper, *Life of Evelyn Underhill*. Longmans, 1958, p. 200
3. Julia de Beausobre, *Flame in the Snow*. Constable, 1945, p. 116

NOTES TO CHAPTER 7

1. *Spirituality for Today*, pp. 172–3
2. Ibid. p. 174
3. E. J. Tinsley, "Parable, Allegory and Mysticism," in *Vindications*, ed. Anthony Hanson. S.C.M., 1966, p. 189
4. *Theological Colleges for Tomorrow*. p. 3
5. *Spirituality for Today*, p. 22
6. *The Vision*, January–June, 1968, p. 11
7. *Spirituality for Today*, p. 11
8. Karl Rahner, *Spiritual Exercises*. Sheed and Ward, 1967, pp. 19–20
9. T. R. Miles, *Religion and the Scientific Outlook*. Allen and Unwin, 1959, p. 74
10. St John of the Cross, op. cit., Vol. III, p. 193
11. Père Grou, *How to Pray*. James Clarke, 1955, p. 48
12. Walter Hilton, *The Ladder of Perfection*, tr. L. Sherley-Price. Penguin Books, 1957, p. 146
13. *Spirituality for Today*, p. 24
14. *Vindications*, p. 158
15. *Ladder of Perfection*, p. 110

16. *How to Pray*, p. 50
17. Ibid. p. 82
18. T. S. Eliot, *Little Gidding*. Faber, 1942, p. 16

NOTES TO CHAPTER 8

1. *The Creative Process*, ed. Brewster Ghiselin. University of California Press, 1952, p. 125
2. J. W. N. Sullivan, *The Limitations of Science*. F. Muller, 1957, p. 2
3. Rostrevor Hamilton, *Poetry and Contemplation*. C.U.P., 1937, pp. 68–9
4. Ibid. p. 77
5. Bradley, *Oxford Lectures on Poetry*. O.U.P., 1909, pp. 4–5
6. *Creativity in the Arts*, ed. Vincent Tomas. Prentice-Hall, 1964, p. 58
7. *Proceedings of Fifth Utah Creativity Research Conference*, ed. C. W. Taylor. U.S.A., 1964, Chapter 8, p. 92
8. Ibid. p. 91
9. *Creativity in the Arts*, p. 51
10. Ibid. p. 73
11. *The Creative Process*, p. 114
12. Ibid. p. 189
13. Ibid. p. 47
14. *What is Mysticism?*, p. 21
15. Harold Shapiro, Article: "The Musical Mind." Winter, 1946
16. *Creativity Research Conference Proceedings*, p. 84
17. Dom Aelred Graham, *The Love of God*. Longmans, 1939, p. 123
18. Ben Shahn, in *Creativity in the Arts*, p. 28
19. *What is Mysticism?*, p. 56
20. *The Creative Process*, p. 14
21. Ibid. p. 87
22. Ibid. p. 14
23. *Creativity in the Arts*, p. 59
24. *The Creative Process*, p. 25
25. Evelyn Underhill, *Mysticism*. Methuen, 1911, pp. 172–3
26. St John of the Cross, op. cit. Vol. III, p. 243
27. Jan van Ruysbroeck, *Seven Steps of the Ladder of Spiritual Love*, tr. Sherwood Taylor. Dacre Press, 1943, pp. 55–6
28. *The Creative Process*, p. 18
29. *Creativity Research Conference Proceedings*, p. 83
30. Ibid. p. 84
31. Jacques Maritain, *The Degrees of Knowledge*, tr. Wall and Adamson. Bles, 1937, p. 444
32. *The Creative Process*, p. 57

Notes   117

33. *Creativity in the Arts*, from Ben Shahn, the Biography of a Painting, p. 31
34. *The Creative Process*, from Roger Sessions, "Creativity in Music," p. 489
35. St John of the Cross, op. cit., Vol. I, p. 63
36. Ruysbroeck, *Book of Supreme Truth* (see above), pp. 240–1
37. *The Creative Process*, from Henry Miller, "Reflections on Writing," p. 178
38. St Catharine of Siena, *Dialogue*, tr. Thorold. Newman Press, 1926, c. iv
39. Henry Miller, *Reflections on Writing* (see above), Note 37
40. Ibid.
41. William Gordon, *The Mind and Art of Henry Miller*. Jonathan Cape 1968, p. 197
42. Henry Miller, *Big Sur and the Oranges of Hieronymus Bosch*. New Directions, New York, 1957, pp. 33–4
43. Ibid. p. 268
44. *Henry Miller, the Man and his Works*, ed. George Wickes. Forum House Publishing Company, 1969, p. 192
45. Archimandrite Sofrony, *The Undistorted Image*, tr. R. Edmonds. Faith Press, 1958, p. 37
46. Ibid. p. 123
47. Louis Bouyer, *Introduction to Spirituality*, tr. M. P. Ryan. Desdee Company, 1961, p. 37

NOTES TO CHAPTER 9

1. Eric Mascall, *Corpus Christi*. Longmans, 1953, Rev. 1965, p. 46
2. Louis Bouyer, *Life and Liturgy*. Sheed and Ward, 1956, p. 59
3. Colin Dunlop, *Anglican Public Worship*. S.C.M., 1953, p. 93
4. Louis Bouyer, *Rite and Man*. Burns and Oates, 1963, p. 61
5. Ibid.
6. Sebastian Moore and Kevin Maguire, *The Experience of Prayer*. Darton, Longman & Todd, 1969, p. 8
7. *Spirituality for Today*, p. 122
8. *The Times*, 3 October 1969
9. Charles Morgan,, *The Fountain*. Macmillan, 1932, p. 320
10. Thomas Merton, *Life and Holiness*. Chapman, 1963, p. 13
11. Louis Bouyer, *Doctrinal Commentary on Conciliar Constitution Liturgy*, 1964, p. 44

Index of Names